Joy in the Classroom

Joy in the Classroom

by Stephanie Herzog

Edited by Ann Ray, Ph.D.

UNIVERSITY OF THE TREES PRESS
Boulder Creek, California 95006

Printed in the United States by R.R. Donnelley & Sons Company

Designed by Lisa S. Mirski

Cover photography by Joanne Jonas

Drawings by children from Scotts Valley, CA School District

Library of Congress Cataloging in Publication Data

Herzog, Stephanie, 1947–
   Joy in the classroom.

   1. Perception—Study and teaching.   2. Education of
children. I. Title.
BF723.P36H47   372.8   82-4724
ISBN 0–916438–46–5   AACR2

Dedication

This book is written for teachers everywhere so that they may come to experience joy in the classroom.

It is dedicated to my father, Fred Valentine Herzog, for showing me the wonder of life and for sharing the beauty of his heart with me during the last years of his life.

It is also dedicated to my teacher, Christopher Hills. I thank him for his great love, caring and work for all of humanity and for teaching me the importance of keeping the hero alive in each child. I thank him also for teaching me how to live this life with spontaneity and joy, a gift for which I can never repay him.

Contents

Acknowledgements

I thank Ann Ray for her many hours of editing work, for all her support, encouragement and prodding in creating this book, and for teaching me how to edit my own work. I thank Deborah Rozman for her inspiration and guidance in helping me learn to teach children to meditate and for her feedback on the text of the book. It has been a great privilege to work with both of these wonderful women. Thank you, too, Norah, for sharing your delightful story, "The Happy Spark", which inspired the children so much. And thank you, Shanti, for typing all of the text so beautifully.

Lisa Mirski designed the book and its cover, and I am grateful for her lovely work. My appreciation to Bruce Cryer for his guidance in all the little steps in book production, and to Ary King, Gloria Herrera and all the rest of the great book production team for the hours and love that they devoted to typesetting and paste-up. My thanks also to Joanne Jonas for the fantastic front cover picture, to Michael Hammer for the beautiful pictures of the children, and to Anne Cameron Cutri for her care in the selection of pictures for the text. I also want to thank Linda Parks-Gobets for her help with last-minute typing and Carol Shiboshkaa for hours of transcribing tapes of actual classroom meditations and children's responses.

The writing of this book was modeled after *Teacher*, by Sylvia Ashton Warner, whom I thank for writing a book which inspired me so much during my early years of teaching.

From the Superintendent of Schools

As children face the increased pace of life with the impact of television, computers, increased activities for themselves and their parents, they are bombarded with endless movement, activity and noise. How to cope with these changes is one of the challenges for those who teach and care about our youth.

This challenge was faced by this author in perceiving a way to help children come to greater peace within themselves and, consequently, find ways to extend this peace and sense of well-being to others.

I have experienced children using the centering techniques and have seen the positive results that are gained by the process. Centering techniques should be a part of the teacher's "tools" to help children in their learning.

There is no doubt that the unique concepts offered in this book will help both teachers and children to deal positively with increased pressures on their lives, both for today and for the changing needs of tomorrow. I heartily recommend *Joy in the Classroom*.

DONALD R. SLEZAK, Ed. D.
Superintendent
Scotts Valley Union School District

To the Reader

Stephanie Herzog is one of those rare child-like beings who somehow never loses the innocent loving heart that we see in children when they are very young. To this simple quality of innocence can we attribute her tremendous success in teaching children to love and accept themselves, to pare down their restless superficial egos and become the beautiful people they really are.

When you walk into Stephanie's classroom after she leads the children in meditation, you find not a group of children, but a group of beings. Tight discipline and gentle, loving warmth are visible at the first glance. As you look deeper, you find that Stephanie is talking directly to the being of each child and that the children are relating to each other from a level beyond personality. There are the normal frequent journeys into the world of silliness, teasing, problems, fantasies, and social discussion, but the atmosphere is different from most school classrooms. The children know that they are accepted for who they really are and they are learning to accept each other in the same way. In Stephanie's classroom, children are given the opportunity to let go of comparing the differences between them and to enjoy being the same in heart and feeling. This sameness is not the dullness of conformity but a feeling of oneness, a feeling of experiencing others as oneself.

While a loving, caring and firm teacher will always positively influence her children, meditation added to the classroom transforms the nature of the class by grabbing hold of the very essence of goodness in the child and drawing it out. "Educate" means "to bring out" the knowledge from within. Meditation draws out the goodness, the original virtue lying deep within even the most defensive child. When children feel their own essence being, their own sweetness inside, their soul, whatever name you call it, they find the part of themselves they can love and call their own. To help the child recognize and touch at will that place inside is a great gift. No matter what other feelings they may have about themselves—poor self-image, self-doubt, self-hatred—when they learn how to touch their real self within, they are reclaiming that which they have lost touch with from babyhood, that feeling we all yearn for which confirms that we are all right.

The contented, wide-eyed look we see so often on a baby's face reveals a being who is in touch with itself. Learning occurs extremely rapidly in that state of being in babies whose little brains must navigate the seas of physical objects, coordination, observation, comprehension, language and communication all at the same time—a tremendous task. And learning occurs most rapidly at any age when we are in that same state of peace within ourself. Being at peace is not to be confused with being self-satisfied, which is a closed state of mind that protects itself from more input, but rather being open, ready, expectant to take in more of the wide universe happening in and around our awareness. Meditation re-awakens that open state of learning.

It was many years ago that I discovered this purpose of meditation. I was caring for a two-year-old toddler. One sunny morning he was leading me around outside the house, asking questions one after the other, when I noticed a glow of light about his face and an ecstatic joy beaming from his eyes. I became very quiet, pretending inside myself that I was two years old just like him, opening to his world to receive from him what it felt like. A quiet stillness broke on the shores of my being as I walked behind him. A feeling of wonder bordered that stillness and spread outward as we walked around the back of the house exploring the universe through the eyes of a two-year-old. We were in a garden of delights. I laughed and he laughed with me, turning around to look at me and our joy mingled as a wave of life. I marveled at the light that seemed to be pouring out of his face and all around me.

In that quiet moment so much insight came and settled in my awareness, beyond thoughts, and I knew that every child had the birthright to keep that sacred experience of being a child at the heart of their existence, and I also knew that meditation was the way by which they could stay in touch with that center of their self throughout life. With a sense of eternal conviction I knew that bringing meditation to children, and finding the way that would be suitable to teach it to them, was the most important thing to do on the whole planet.

From that day, I began to ponder on ways that would help people consciously recontact that childlike wonder within, that place we touch whenever we feel truly spontaneous, fulfilled, at one inside ourself. Through experimenting with children of many ages to find what techniques of getting in touch worked, their different stages of growth and different learning challenges became apparent to me. But with all the moods, interests, personalities, attention spans and ages, one common denominator remained—whenever a child became truly still and quiet in himself, a sweetness and selflessness would come out, and even radiate from his being.

Like the angelic expression many children have when they are asleep, meditation would bring about a different vibrational presence to the children. The atmosphere is more than the mere absence of noise or movement; it is a stillness that comes from being at peace with oneself. And I began to find that whatever task the children did following the period of true quiet, was done with a greater completeness of attention, a greater receptivity and spontaneous creativity than at any other time. The activity was performed like a well-greased bicycle, with all the parts working harmoniously together. And the children seemed to enjoy whatever they did then, working together well from a deeper, more fulfilled part of themselves.

From these early experiments evolved several years of research and application of techniques to teach children how to meditate, how to quiet their bodies and emotions and find their still center of being within many different settings. Several public school districts sponsored research, and from this my first book, *Meditating With Children: The Art of Concentration and Centering,* was written. When I published the book in 1976, I felt that it would reach those teachers who were searching for something that would change their daily lives and make teaching more like the ideals they had had in mind when they first entered the profession. I always envisioned that creative teachers would take the techniques that I had developed and would not only change the lives of many children with them, but would write their own books which would reach far and wide to help other teachers, parents and children transform their lives. So I am very fulfilled, seeing this new book, *Joy in the Classroom,* springing from the seed I planted six years ago.

It was during a series of in-service trainings following the book's publication, that I met Stephanie Herzog. Stephanie is one of those teachers who can take a technique and because of her conviction, can bring out its best with children. Without letup, Stephanie has pioneered the use of meditation in the public school classroom, in a traditional and highly conservative school district. Surmounting parent concern, adminstrative scrutiny, and the reactions of some highly disturbed children, Stephanie, undaunted in what she was doing, has demonstrated that it can be done anywhere. The testimony for all has been the joyful faces of her children year after year, their rapid academic and social learning and, eventually, grateful parents.

In *Joy in the Classroom* Stephanie shares her struggles and joys of pioneering a new way of teaching in a classic public school and offers what she has distilled as a gift to other educators, parents and friends of children, that they might also learn to experience that communing with their own beings and with the being of the child as the first step of true education, real learning, and fulfilling teaching. Having broken the ground, *Joy in the Classroom* is certain to be the cornerstone for a new foundation in teacher training.

DEBORAH ROZMAN, Ph.D.

Tuning into the center.

CHAPTER 1

How I Began
To Teach Meditation

I began teaching twelve years ago. Early in my student teaching experience, a question rose up from my innermost being: how does a teacher get a group of youngsters to listen and follow directions with the minimal amount of shouting and punitive action and the maximum amount of warmth and joy? As the years passed, the question seemed to become increasingly relevant and complex. Problem students seemed to be on the increase. Hyperactivity, lack of concentration, uncaring for others, disrespect for peers and adults became more and more the norm. What does one do with the student who has so much frustration built up inside that he yanks hair out of the head of another child every time he gets angry? How do you teach a second-grader to read when he can't concentrate more than one minute even though you are giving him personal one-to-one attention? Where were the answers? I began a hearty search.

I began attending any class on classroom discipline and management I could find. Class meetings, active listening, logical consequences, and positive incentives soon became part of my regular curriculum. These techinques worked with a reasonable amount of success, and at this point I gave up looking for discipline techniques. This was about six years ago. Great thinkers have said that when you give up your attachment to something, it comes to you; when you give up trying, all things come easily. This seemed to happen to me. In October of that same year, I went to a school district in-service workshop, expecting to sit half-bored for three hours and come away with little that could be actually applied in the classroom. Instead, it was the turning point in my life as a teacher of children.

I can't remember anything about any of the speakers that day except for Deborah Rozman. It was not her pleasant looks or her words or manner of speaking (although these were excellent) that made the difference. It was her being. She was radiant and seemed at peace with herself. She spoke about teaching children to meditate, something unheard of in public school teaching. Could meditation teach children to concentrate better? Would my students really begin to use more than ten percent of their brains? What creative potential would be released? Thrilled by the possibilities of what meditation might do for my students, I began to teach it the very next day.

This book is about what happened that year and during the two years following. It is written especially for teachers who are courageous enough to take a risk and try something new. It is for the teacher who wants to learn to speak directly to the hearts of students and who is not afraid to express real love.

The day after the in-service workshop I walked into the classroom knowing I was going to teach meditation for the first time to the children. Many questions and doubts danced in my mind. Would the children respond to it positively? Would they all try to stay quiet with eyes closed? Would their parents call the principal and complain that I was teaching religion? My doubts and fears dissolved almost immediately. The children responded quite well to the challenge of keeping bodies and eyes still for a few minutes. The walls of the administration and throngs of angry parents did not come crashing down on my head.

That first morning I gathered my second grade children into a circle around me and told them we were going to do an exercise that would give them more energy for their work and help them concentrate better. I had them close their eyes and relax all their body parts, breathe quietly five times, and concentrate for awhile on a star between their eyes while imagining having a good day and doing the very best they could on all their work. After the exercise I had them tense their bodies to bring themselves back and then I had them open their eyes. The children sat very quietly for a few minutes. Then I asked them to go to their activity centers and start their work as usual.

Now, on any normal morning some children would not go straight to work. A few would meander around or visit a friend until I reminded them. But on this day, immediately following the centering exercise the whole class went quietly to work and was fully absorbed until noon. Usually after a few hours the children began to get restless and have trouble concentrating. This morning was different. For the first time the children were deeply focused and stayed zeroed in on what they were doing. The results proved to be consistent. From then on, each morning we did the same routine followed by the children going quietly to work, usually being able to stay centered for the rest of the morning. I began to enjoy teaching in a way I never had before and found myself looking forward to coming to class. Generally, teachers in today's public schools expect a hectic day. But now my class radiated a peaceful energy that flowed into me. I, in turn, would start to radiate a peaceful feeling, and it would all multiply. For the first time, teaching became a completely joyful experience.

Going quietly to work.

CHAPTER 2

Why Did Meditation Help the Children Become More Responsible?

Meditation* is a technique for getting in touch with our own inner wisdom. Most children grow up without ever discovering that there is a source of wisdom and strength and love inside themselves. They look to their parents for these qualities, but often parents are lacking in these qualities themselves. Even if they have them, can you really give those qualities to another person? They must be discovered inside of ourselves. Those who are wise with another person's wisdom are always off center, unsure of who *they* are. Meditation helps us find our *own* center and to know our own selves as we really are—not as someone else tells us we are. So you can see how important it could be in the lives of those children whose parents tell them they are stupid or ugly or program into the child's sensitive mind some other negative quality. Most of us carry throughout our lives the labels others put on us and we believe that this is who we are. For anyone who is curious to know who he or she *really* is, meditation is the instrument of self-knowledge.

Each thing in nature grows from a seed of some kind. A carrot seed grows into a carrot; an acorn grows into an oak. The "real self" of the oak is contained in that acorn and it cannot become any other kind of tree than what it is. So too, each person has a unique self which is then

---

*The words "meditation" and "centering" are used interchangeably throughout this book and mean the same thing. Whenever I or the children refer to centering we are talking about meditation.

shaped by family, society and life. Sometimes the shaping and training is an improvement, but only if it brings out the true nature of the child. Often it tries to do the opposite and make all children just alike even though, inside, each one is unique. If you spend time trying to coach the carrot into being more like the oak tree, then the carrot will develop a deep inner conflict, or perhaps become ill, because each thing has an inherent need to be itself.

This was the message of the story of the ugly duckling. He was criticized by the other ducks for being different, and he felt terrible about himself until one day, he came upon a lake full of swans and discovered that he was not a duck at all but a swan and that although he had been an ugly duck, he was, as a swan, just what he should be. He felt the joy of being at one with himself, no longer subject to the opinions of others. No matter what they might say, he now knew what he was, and no one could take it from him ever again.

This is what meditation does for children and adults alike—it brings them to this joy of knowing who they really are. Meditation is not introspection or a kind of thinking process but is just learning to be still. In the stillness we are able to perceive what is normally covered up in the clamor and bustle and conflict of life.

Learning to be still.

Unfortunately in education, much of the discipline for children has come from outside themselves, from a teacher or parent telling them what to do. This does not allow the child to develop his or her own inner authority. Responsibility does not come from outside oneself. Many of us have grown up without learning to use our own inner sense of wisdom and right action. We may still look for authority from books, speakers, and T.V. Real authority comes from the deep center of knowing what's right. We can tune in and feel inside whether an action is really the right action for us or not.

After using meditation in my classes, I began to notice a definite change in the students' ability to be self-disciplined, self-motivating, and responsible. I don't think the children in my class were conscious that they were gaining these qualities and it was not an intention of mine to accomplish this through meditation. It all just happened naturally. It was as if tuning to their deep inner center of stillness on a daily basis helped them to create that sense of centeredness in all their actions.

One way the children became more responsible was that they would get themselves ready for centering and other classroom activities without my having to ask them. As they came into the room from recess I would often hear them whispering to one another, "Let's surprise teacher by having our heads down on our desks." Before an activity they would say, "Hurry up, let's get ready before teacher gets here."

The children maintained a sense of responsibility, whether I was in charge of them or not. Substitute teachers often commented on how easy the children were to work with. One Halloween I called for a substitute to work part of the morning so I could go to a doctor because I could not see out of my right eye. When I returned to class, the substitute expressed what a pleasure it was to work with the class. It was Halloween, a time when children are usually pretty wound-up, but she found the children quiet and cooperative.

Many substitutes who worked in my class during the three years I taught meditation at Brook Knoll School, left notes expressing that they would like to come back and work with the children again. As Tom Brentwood put it, "Had an easy day that was very enjoyable.

Would be glad to work here again, if the need arises." It was interesting to get these notes because two of the three years I was teaching meditation I was supposedly teaching classes which had many discipline problems.

One thing I discovered that you should not do, however, with substitutes is to have them lead the centering, especially if they have never done so before. The children will become used to the way you lead centering. Substitutes who worked with my class always changed the wording a bit from the way I led it. This would always result in the children bursting into peals of laughter. When you cannot be at school have one of your students lead the centering. The children are much more receptive to being led in the centering process by one of their classmates than by a stranger. The children usually do a pretty good job of leading it. They can really surprise you.

In regard to the children growing more responsible, what sticks out the most in my mind is rainy days. Rainy days had always been a source of frustration and exhaustion for me, with no recesses and a long lunch hour with children so full of restlessness and bound-up energy. I dreaded rainy days and we had a lot of them since we were living in the Santa Cruz mountains. We could have up to eighty inches of rain in a single winter. One winter it rained nearly thirty days straight. It wasn't any gentle rain either. I recall dreading the walk from my classroom to the office because the rain came down like a waterfall off the ends of the building. There was no covered walkway for protection! When it rained, there was no place for the children to be except the classroom. We had no gymnasium or cafeteria. On rainy days we were stuck in one place all day. We studied, ate lunch, exercised, and played all in the same space. You can imagine the children's energy at the end of the day. I always went home exhausted on rainy days, dreading the next, hoping the sky would break forth into bright sun.

In this rainy season we had "yard duties" to cover the children at lunch time. Usually a "yard duty" had charge of six classrooms, walking from classroom to classroom trying to keep order. But they did not necessarily know the children or the class dynamic well enough to be able to discipline a class if the children became disruptive. Since the children in each class knew that the yard duty did not know how things really ran in that class, it was not uncommon for the children to become disruptive at lunch time. We were often called from the teachers' room by the "yard duties" because they could not control the children. Many of the teachers of the younger children (myself included) began to eat with their classes all through the lunch hour on rainy days to help keep order. I found I was often asked by the "yard duties" to help with discipline in nearby classrooms where teachers did not stay.

During the first year of using meditation in the classroom I began to notice the children in my class becoming more responsible during the lunch hours on rainy days. They began to become self-directed during these times, choosing from different games and activities in the room and staying absorbed in them. It would have been hard for an onlooker to tell if it was lunch time or a regular classroom activity time. Some children might be engrossed in building a tower with the large blocks in one corner of the room. A few other children might choose to color. Some might be playing a game of chess or checkers. Another group of boys and girls together might be playing house behind the large bookshelf in the back of the room. I began to be able to go down to the teachers' room to eat lunch or run off dittos without being interrupted because some disruption had arisen which the "yard duties" couldn't deal with.

The "yard duty" people began to notice the change in my students as well. They began to express how they felt about walking into a class which was orderly and well-behaved. Kathy, a new instructional aide, expressed how pleased and surprised she was to find my class playing cooperatively one Friday afternoon. Here is what she observed:

> *"Last rainy day Friday I kept check on all the classrooms.*
> *What a pleasant surprise to walk into your class and the*
> *children were so quiet and peaceful. Just on my*
> *observation they seemed so at peace and it was all*
> *self-directed, there weren't any adults around. None*
> *of the other classes came even close to being so centered.*
> *What a pleasure, what a wonderful gift!"*

The children began to become more responsible at recess time as well as on rainy days. During the second year of teaching meditation to children I found the class was able to do something none of my classes of young children were able to do before. They were able to play "7-up" at recess time alone by themselves. One child led the game. It was great because Tanya, my instructional aide, and I were able to get work done. We only had to intervene now and then.

On January 5, 1978, due to a big storm with high winds and driving rains, the lights went out at lunch time. My class was the only class in our wing of the school which did not burst out screaming. The lights kept going out so we spent the afternoon telling jokes, riddles, and stories. We all sat around on our big blue centering rug in a circle in the dark. It was quite dark because of the storm outside. Our circle became smaller and smaller and more intimate. Wonderful feelings of love and closeness filled the room. The children did not get scared or feel uncomfortable because the lights were out. They seemed to have a lot of control.

A few days later the lights went out again while we were centering. We had just finished relaxation and breathing. Some of the children started giggling. Others became upset and said, "Stop it, we're trying to relax." The majority of children seemed intent on finishing the meditation, so we continued the exercise by sending good thoughts, love and energy to one another. Following that, we surrounded ourselves with good energy.

What caused my students to become more responsible? Responsible means "ability to respond". My students were certainly responding and seemed to have learned to respond in a positive way to exciting and, what to some children could have been, upsetting situations. In the past I had had children burst out crying or call out for their mothers when the lights went out in a class. The children who had been meditating seemed to be able to come from a more secure state of being when things happened which could have been disturbing to them. They were more in control of themselves from within and not so controlled by outside circumstances.

For example, one morning an announcement came over the loudspeakers during our meditation. I asked the children to keep their eyes closed, which they did. We were able to continue the meditation uninterrupted. It was amazing to see what self-control they had.

At the end of the second year that I taught meditation to children, we went to Alan's house to swim for an end-of-the-year party. I was concerned about having so many children around a swimming pool. Again, I was surprised to see how responsibly the children behaved. There was no pushing or fighting. At first everyone swam. Then the children wandered off naturally into other activities—sunbathing, playing ball, etc. They were all quite self-directed. Anna, Eva, Anthony and Cary all wanted to learn to swim. What energy and enthusiasm they had! Roger became chilled and quietly took care of himself by finding a warm spot in the sun to lie down. The children were so responsible that we adults were able to enjoy one another's company. It was a real treat!

Rema Stone, a parent who worked as a parent volunteer, had this to say about the children's sense of responsibility:

> *"While helping in your class one day I was pleased to note how well 'all' of the children joined in when it was time to 'center' and how well they worked together afterwards. I had never seen such cooperation before or since in a classroom."*

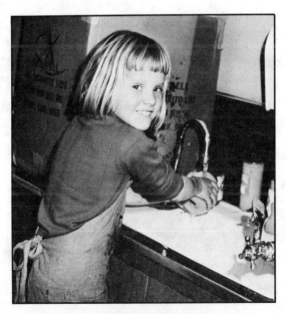

Responsibility can be fun.

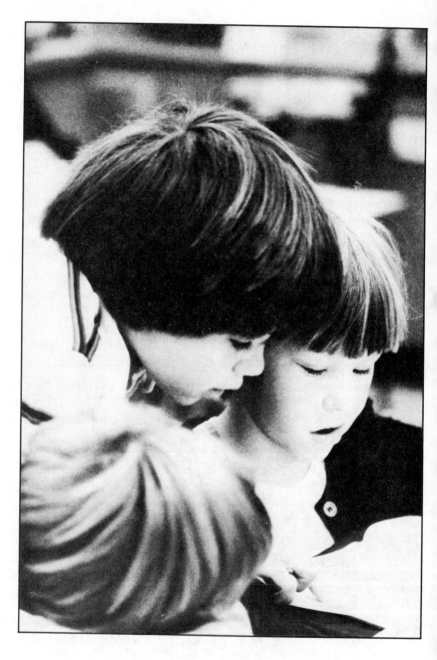

Working together

CHAPTER 3

Why Teach Meditation
In the Classroom?

After using meditation for awhile during
my first year teaching it, I began to tell some
of the other teachers about it. I recall visiting
Freida, the teacher who taught next door to
me, sharing the wonderful results I was
having with it, suggesting she try it. She and I
both had discipline problems that year. Her
class was even harder than mine to control.
"The centering might calm down some of
your students," I suggested. Freida responded to my sharing with
skepticism, and I knew she would never try it. I told Dr. Slezak, my
superintendent, how painful it was to have discovered something that
really worked and to have other teachers doubt it and keep on
struggling with their old ways. He commented that many times
teachers do not recognize a good thing when it comes out of their own
school system. They are looking for authorities and do not consider a
fellow teacher worth listening to. He said that they would listen to a
teacher who came from another school district to share something
new. After that I no longer encouraged other teachers to try it, but let
them be.

One of the sixth-grade teachers, however, did become curious and
began to ask me questions about what I was doing. The next year she
decided to try it with her sixth-graders. After that we had many
sharings about what we were doing. It was great to have someone to
talk with. She gave a reward every Friday to the row that did the best
job of being quiet while centering. She discovered that her older

students preferred silent meditations to guided ones. She, herself, began to center daily before school, at lunch time, and before she went to bed. She said it was like focusing a fuzzy camera: "Once all my scattered thoughts are out of the way, my mind becomes like a focused camera, all sharp and zeroed in." She also said that if she breathed in love when she was upset with students, she could handle them and their problems from a more centered place.

During the second year I taught meditation, an article I wrote appeared in *New Age Journal* entitled, "Meditation for Children," describing my first year teaching meditation. After reading the article, another teacher, a friend of mine named Margie, decided to try the centering technique. On that day, her children came in from eleven o'clock recess in a noisy way. Being angry at one another, some children were name-calling across the room. She led them through centering and had them imagine they were a balloon which got so big it was full of all the love they had inside. Then she had them think of one person who had been kind to them in the room. After the centering the class was calm and quiet, quite different from the noisy boisterous state they were in before recess. A wonderful discussion followed, the children saying things like, "I appreciate John because he plays with me." The whole class vibration had changed from name-calling to the children appreciating one another. They expressed appreciation for their teacher also, saying, "I like the way you help us," and for their adopted grandfather (an elderly man who volunteered in the school), "We like the way you play with us." Afterwards they all went quietly to the library. Margie's face sparkled with excitement as she told me about this transformation.

If you have ever thought of using meditation in your classroom, your thoughts may have run as follows: "My day is already too full of subjects to cover. Is it really worth the challenge of getting thirty youngsters perfectly quiet for a few minutes each day?" If your experience of the classroom is anything like mine, the answer is "Yes! Well worth it." I am finding that teaching becomes a more challenging profession each year. The tensions and anxieties of our increasingly fast-paced society are not only affecting us, they are also affecting our children. In my twelve years of experience in the classroom, I have observed in children a tremendous increase in hyperactivity, hyper-tension, anger, depression, lack of concentration, lack of self-worth, and disrespect for peers, adults, and property. Parents are either unwilling or unable to discipline their own children, so they look to us as teachers to be the "miracle workers" who will whip them into shape. It always amazes me on field trips how many parents cannot control their own children—the children running about wildly while the parent screams and shouts helplessly.

In my experience, more and more parents of very young children are both working in order to meet the financial crunch, so they are leaving their children to fend for themselves during sizeable amounts of time both day and night. Many of these children are left to roam the streets, getting into mischief. Often children share with me the pain and loneliness this causes them. Repeatedly I am shocked to touch a second-grader on the shoulders and discover the muscles tied up in knots of tension. Many children are so riddled with tension, anxiety, hyperactivity, boredom, loneliness, frustration and anger that *they cannot learn*. An angry, depressed child cannot concentrate. He is using all his energy to hold in negative feelings. A child whose emotions are out of control feels helpless and depressed. His body does not feel good. It is important to know that tense, hyperactive and angry children are not bad; they just do not know how to control themselves. The first step in learning to release anger is relaxation. Meditation in the classroom provides a safe, non-threatening avenue in which the tense, angry, or hyperactive student can relax the body and then let go of negative emotions. This is because a child must be at a deeper conscious level to actually change his emotions. Meditation helps the child experience that deeper level. Relaxation and deep breathing, the first two steps in meditation, are major keys. No negative emotion can be released as long as a person is tense and holding on to it. It is important to have the child get in touch with feelings before beginning deep breathing, because you will then encourage him to let go of any negative emotions, as he breathes, by allowing them to float out on the outbreath. By constant practice of these steps the child learns he can control and change his emotions, especially in difficult situations.

Of course, not all children are angry or hyperactive. But they do all have emotions, even though they may not share them with you unless you have made an avenue for that kind of sharing. We do not give children much opportunity in our schools to listen to themselves. We spend a lot of time talking to them, leading discussions, and creating numerous stimulating external learning situations. This is because we ourselves spend little time listening to our bodies, to our feelings, and to our thoughts. But children who learn to listen to themselves become more certain of themselves. I have found that childrens' awareness of their own feelings and the feelings of others increases through daily practice in meditation. A beautiful sensitive caring begins to flow between the children. Because they begin to listen to their own inner feelings, they are more capable of listening to the feelings of another. One parent observed the following growth in self-awareness in her daughter: "I have seen her remove herself from a stressful situation and use the centering techniques. She also seems to have an added 'self-awareness' as she says centering helps her know how she feels."

Who is this centered self? Who and what are human beings anyway? Each new day new discoveries are being made into the fantastic abilities of our brains, minds, and bodies. Studies show that people are only using about 10% of their physical potential and 5% of their mental potential. What would life be like if we were using our *full* potential? How can such potential be tapped? Men and women are much more than bodies and minds; we are also our intuition, imagination, heart, soul, and social awareness. God only knows what we are really capable of! But are we teaching the children in our schools to manifest their fantastic potential? Absolutely not! The higher levels of functioning and communicating are not demanded or supported by our society or our education system. We are still educating as we did in the late nineteenth century, even though the world we live in has totally changed.

Basically cognitive, linear, and analytical learning is still the main stress in our schools along with some physical training. Many teachers are still too set in their certain and secure ways of dealing with children to break away and try new techniques. But the need is screaming at us. Linear, cognitive education cripples the child. To know "about" is much different than to know. How many of the facts you memorized in school stick in your mind? Or do you remember instead the essence, the feeling vibration of what it was like to be in so-and-so's class? What is really important to you now? Is it all those facts you memorized? Or are you more concerned with how you are getting along with husband or wife, whether you will be loved tomorrow, or how you are going to cover all the bills next month? Did school really give you much that you can apply practically now in daily life? Did anyone teach you how to use your consciousness—that fantastic equipment you received at birth? The answer is simply no. And today we are still doing little to train children to use their consciousness. In fact we are teaching basically only half of their brain—the left hemisphere of the brain. When are we going to take the limits off education and teach the whole child, including his intuition, imagination, and true creative potential?

I believe that meditation used daily in the classroom can help to fill the enormous gap found in today's education. Meditation stimulates the right hemisphere of the child's brain in a natural and wholistic way. Actually your right and left brain hemispheres are combined with the heaviest fibers in your body. They are interconnected and work together. More learning occurs if both hemispheres are stimulated and are working. Imagine the crippling effect on both hemispheres which occurs when only one hemisphere is stimulated in our present educational system.

The left hemisphere is sequential and temporal. It makes the statement, "If this, then that." The left hemisphere analyzes and looks at things in parts instead as a whole. It governs counting and speech and handles details and interprets words. The right hemisphere of the brain governs the intuition, imagination, and creativity. It is the visual, spatial hemisphere which puts things together in wholes—sees the whole thing at once. Farmers, artists, and musicians make use of their right hemisphere. Music is interpreted in the right hemisphere. Your right hemisphere tells you if someone is upset with you by the tone of their voice. Your left hemisphere analyzes a person's words, while your right hemisphere interprets their angry face.

Children are natural visualizers; they usually think in vivid images. A child you are teaching right now in your classroom may have fantastic art or music going on in his head that you aren't aware of. Most of this natural right brain activity dies in a person before adulthood. Images are very important in our lives because they mobilize us for action, giving us the enthusiasm and hormonal build-up necessary to complete a task. Have you ever wondered why children have so much energy? Could it be that their images and visions may be producing that spark, that wondrous lust for life to be experienced here and now? Meditation opens the door in a natural way to the child's creative imagination and natural visualizing process governed by the right hemisphere of the brain. I have found that through meditation, the children's verbal, written, and artistic expression become increasingly exciting, more detailed, and more expressive. The children appear to be tapping into the same pool of creative images that artists, poets, and visionaries draw from. Their images are full of light and color—ever-changing and beautiful. The maturity with which children are able to express their experiences is also incredible. Beautiful stories emerge from the children's meditations—with beginnings, middles, and endings. Children who at seven years old do not normally fill in a whole page with color, after meditating for awhile, suddenly do so. Fantastic drawings and paintings in brilliant colors emerge. And you as a teacher no longer have to prod and encourage children to write creatively; the content flows out of them easily and naturally. True learning occurs when it is drawn out of the child's own fantastic potential.

My experience has been that meditation helps students find peace, wisdom, and strength by discovering an inner world of inspiration. The child no longer has to look outside himself for authority, security, and confirmation. He becomes self-directed, much more able to make his own decisions. He solves problems more through discussion of feelings than through fighting. He gains control over his body, emotions, and mind. As the child feels more in control of himself, he has more control over his environment and doesn't feel as victimized.

For example, a child named Anthony entered my second-grade class with a very low self-image. Academically he was not doing well. During first grade he was the victim of other children's cruel teasing. They called him "flat face" and other names which immediately put him into a rage of anger. Being a very physical child he would respond with fists flying, and a hot and heavy fight would ensue. Anthony was a helpless victim of his own anger. Since the other children knew they could elicit this response by name calling they continued to call him names, and Anthony continued to find himself a victim of circumstances out of his control. I recall the other second-grade teacher telling me she was glad she didn't have Anthony as a student because he was so "hard to handle".

From the very beginning, Anthony liked meditation. On the first day of school I led the class on a journey in their spaceships out into outer space, looking for the end of the universe. We whizzed past the moon, sun, the planets and stars. Upon opening his eyes, Anthony said, "Wow!" In his imagination he had seen all the planets in vivid colors of yellow, red, and orange.

Child's drawing.

A few months after his participating in meditation I began to observe definite changes in Anthony. He seemed to be gaining a certain sense of self-confidence. He was having fewer fights out on the yard. His eyes often sparkled with joy and delight in class. One day, after afternoon meditation, as we were sharing feelings, Anthony said, "I really like this class because no one here calls me flat face. Last year the kids always called me names and I got into fights. Now I don't have to fight anymore because it doesn't matter if they call me names.

They're not true anyway."

Anthony by this time had become aware of the fact that he did not have to respond to name calling in the same old ways. As a result he was no longer a helpless victim of the other children. Realizing that they could no longer knock Anthony off his centered self and elicit his anger, they gave up calling him names on the yard. Through tuning in to his inner self, Anthony had found a new conviction in his own worth which he carried both inside and outside the classroom. His mother confirmed that the change in him was also evident at home. She was so pleased with it that she and her husband began to take classes in the meditation process themselves.

Anthony also began to tackle academic work with enthusiasm, much of it quite a challenge for him to do. From the time he entered kindergarten he had had difficulty learning to read. He also had problems with writing and spelling and, because of this, he spent several hours a day in a special education class. He had been attending the special education class since first grade, but his progress academically was extremely slow. With the new-found confidence that Anthony gained through meditation, he began to put more effort into academic tasks that he previously shied away from. He began to learn to read, at a pace which surprised his special education teacher. He also began to write a few simple sentences. Previous to this he would often refuse to do any type of writing at all. He now began to actually enjoy writing. On the opposite page is a story Anthony wrote in the third grade. Much effort and love went into the writing of this simple story.

If Anthony hadn't been in my class and been exposed to meditation, I don't know if anyone would ever have seen his real being (he had such a terrible reputation among the teachers), and I also am not sure he would ever have found his own self-worth. Moreover, as long as all that rejection was happening at the social level, I don't think he would ever have felt good enough about himself to make progress academically.

Of course, not all children have such difficult problems to master as Anthony did. Monica and Laura were two second-graders who were

Everybody came around to draw pictures of me and the bee and the butterfly. They landed on me.

very stable and normal. Nevertheless, meditation helped them to reach a level of self-mastery which children rarely attain, and for that matter, few adults ever attain it either. Seven-year-old Monica was a foster child living with a large family. One of the older boys, Frank, jumped up and broke a light bulb during the evening meal scattering glass all over the fresh homemade pie. The father began yelling and scolding. Monica was quite upset by the whole incident, taking her father's anger personally, feeling like she had somehow done something bad. She quietly slipped away from the table and into her bedroom, where she led herself through the first few steps of meditation. Here is what she shared about her meditation. "Every bad feeling went out of my body and I had a lot more love, I felt much better." She then proceeded to rejoin the family only to discover her foster father was not really angry at her but was angry because the light had been broken.

During February of 1978 we had some very heavy winter storms with driving rain and winds. One wintery stormy evening, Laura, also seven years old, was playing Scrabble with a friend, when suddenly a tree fell on the house. No one was hurt although considerable damage was done, and the family was stunned. Quite shaken, Laura took her friend into the bedroom and led her through a meditation. She explained to the class the next morning, "We imagined we were safe and no more trees would fall on the house. We felt a lot safer afterwards." Both Monica and Laura were able, because of regular daily practice, to use meditation to change and get mastery over their emotions in difficult situations. They were then able to go back to the situation and respond to it from a more centered, self-assured, calm inner space. Imagine what could happen to our schools if all children learned to respond to challenging circumstances from their centered selves.

Not all the transformations brought about by meditation were gradual, as in the case of Anthony, Monica, and Laura. For a girl named Danielle meditation was so uplifting that she would, within minutes, change dramatically from one state of consciousness to a totally different state of consciousness.

Danielle entered my third-grade class riddled with hostility and fear of rejection. Her original mother had not wanted her and had given her to an aunt to raise. This aunt decided after seven years that she no longer wanted Danielle and sent her from Illinois to California to be raised by yet another aunt. When Danielle began school in my class she was so bound in her emotions she was very hard to teach. She approached each new academic task with loud, disruptive, angry shouts, "This is too hard" or "I can't do this," though actually she was a very bright girl. Out on the playground she fought constantly with her peers, fights which often started with name-calling and ended up with physical hitting. Meditation became a source of renewal for Danielle. Often she came in from lunch recess angry from happenings on the playground. She would join us in the meditation circle with a glum face. But many times after afternoon meditation her countenance and attitude would become totally transformed. It was a very powerful thing to witness. She would then be in a positive frame of mind, excited to share her experience in meditation. In her meditations she got in touch with beautiful images. She enjoyed expressing these in art and writing. During meditation she also got in touch with a beautiful warm caring quality which lay beneath all her negativity. As the school year passed, the whole class benefited from and enjoyed these qualities in Danielle, as she began to share them more and more with the class. Not that participation in meditation cured all of Danielle's problems. By the end of the school year she had not totally mastered her negativity, but she had come a long way.

When Danielle was out on the playground, every problem that arose was the other person's fault. Danielle's natural defense mechanism was to blame the other person, so that she would not have to look at how she created or helped to create the situation. But after meditation, she would be loving towards the very people she had been blaming. Why? Because there was no longer any need to defend. She had melted into the vulnerable state of consciousness that meditation brings—that state in which the heart just loves and doesn't worry about what others will think or do. All babies are born into this sweet vulnerable state of the heart. It is only when they get hurt that they start to build defenses to protect themselves, because it is too painful to be so vulnerable. But ironically, the defenses only bring more pain, because they tend to bring rejection by others.

A boy named Peter had built up an enormous network of defenses before he entered my class as a third-grader—so much so that when I would come up to him or try to strike up a conversation, he wouldn't even talk. Usually he would just grunt one word. In effect he had walled himself up inside a protective wall of silence. At the beginning of the school year he was the most unhappy boy in the class. He always sat looking up at me with a serious look on his face, pain in his eyes, a grim appearance. He didn't relate well to other students. He wasn't enthused about much of anything, nor was he doing well academically. Reading and math were the worst areas for him. Even though he worked very hard, putting much pressure on himself, he seemed always to defeat himself. No matter which girls were in his group, he would pick a fight with them over one thing or another. He'd call them ugly names. The girls would get so upset they would ask to be moved to another group in the classroom.

After several months of centering I began to notice wonderful changes in Peter. His face would soften and lighten up during meditation and it would last through the classroom activities. This melting of inner defenses helped him relate better to the other students. Soon I no longer had to keep moving girls out of his group. His class work improved markedly too. Peter became a fluent reader, proud of his progress, and made nice gains in math work as well. Peter also became one of the best cursive writers in the class. No one was more surprised with Peter's progress than his mother. One of the most delightful changes was that Peter began to talk and share his world with us. He began to smile and share really personal things, like stories about his dog. Once Peter had let down his inner defenses and allowed himself to become vulnerable in this way, he began to express the softer, more sensitive side of his nature, and he no longer felt the need to reject it by striking out at the girls.

As we have seen, the more emotionally balanced the child becomes, the easier it is for him to learn. This is an indirect effect that meditation has on the learning of reading, writing, spelling, math, science, etc. Meditation also develops the art of concentration, which *directly* affects both teaching and learning and without which true learning cannot occur. And yet concentration is a rare skill. Are you aware that most adults cannot concentrate for more than fifteen seconds at a time without the mind darting away with distracting thoughts? Take five minutes right now yourself and see how long you can concentrate on the second hand of a clock without thinking about anything else. Start over each time you find your mind wandering. The ability to concentrate (or to focus the attention on any one thing for a duration of time) is directly proportional to the amount of true learning that can take place in an individual. Meditation teaches the child wonderful concentration.

Alan came to me as a second-grader. He was a large boy and was not doing well academically. He had had a rough time in first grade both academically and socially. He did not feel very good about himself and wanted very much to be accepted by his peers (who rejected him). He was clumsy and often became too rough in playing with other children, not understanding how this upset them and separated them from him. His first-grade teacher had wanted to keep him back another year but had sent him on to second grade because of his size. Upon entry in my class Alan could hardly read a pre-primer, could not print legibly, had no understanding of mathematics, and could not write a sentence.

I had an interesting experience that year because I had about eleven other second-grade students who were reading with difficulty

Here is a sample of Alan's writing upon entering the class. Note that it is impossible to read.

at a pre-primer level. And my school was in a middle to upper-middle class neighborhood, where I hadn't expected such problems. I mustered up all the courage I had and got out all my first-grade materials and expertise (my first three years of teaching had been in first grade). My morning program was basically child-centered learning, with six academic learning stations through which the children rotated within a three hour period. A paid aide, student teacher, and parent volunteer all worked in the learning stations along with me each morning. This allowed for much one-to-one attention with students. I recall working with Alan, trying my very best to help him grasp basic phonetic sounds and math concepts. It was extremely frustrating to work with him because every few minutes his attention would wander someplace else. Often after a twenty-minute period of continually drawing his attention back to the task at hand, I would check to see what he had learned. Virtually nothing! I felt at a loss as to how to help him.

At the start, meditation was very difficult for Alan. He was quite restless and had trouble keeping his body still and eyes closed. It was almost painful to see him struggle each day to try to get his body under control. It was two months before Alan was able to keep his eyes and body still for the first time during the meditation. Afterwards he expressed, "I really felt it going down in my body, the relaxing feeling you were talking about." Alan was very excited about the fact that after two months he now had gained some control over his body and could keep his eyes closed the whole time. During the days which followed he continued to be able to keep his body quiet during meditation. Not long after this, Alan began to take leaps and bounds in academic areas. He began to read all kinds of difficult words. It was as if he had heard and learned everything during all the previous lessons taught him but could not concentrate long enough to show me what he knew. You can imagine the excitement and joy we both experienced. Alan began to grow in self-confidence and began to relate better to his peers. I had Alan as a student in third grade as well. His concentration and attention span continued to improve with daily participation in meditation. By March of his third-grade year Alan's reading word recognition was equal to that of a sixth-grader. He now had the ability to stay focused deeply on a single task for quite a long period of time. After a good hour of concentrated academic work he would sometimes choose to stay in at recess as well, to finish a task.

Here is a sample of Alan's writing during the second half of third grade. Compared to his illegible scribbles upon entering the second grade class, Alan had made a lot of progress.

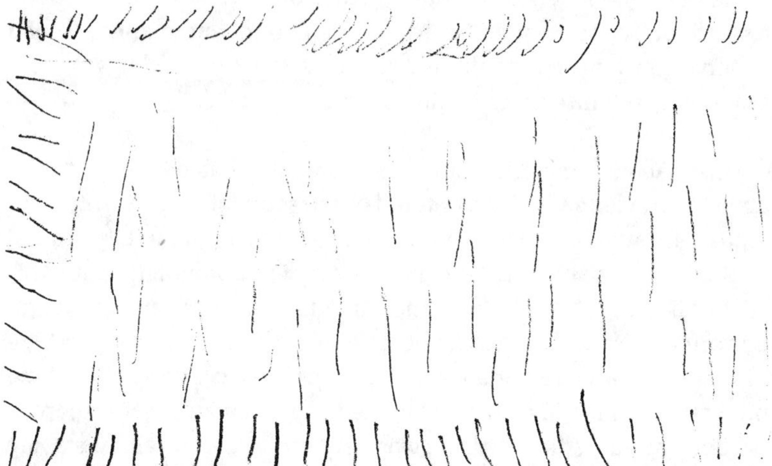

I imagined that I was
in a meadow with
tall grass and long
paths through
the grass and you
could play hid
and go seek and chase.

One morning because of heavy fog I chose to drive up to the school on an alternate back route where there was less traffic. Alan was walking up to school on the same route and did not notice me come up behind him. It warmed my heart to see him walk; there was an air of self-confidence, a certain steady bounce in his walk. When he arrived at school I mentioned the self-confident manner I had observed in him. He confirmed in his own words feelings of self-assurance in himself and in all his work.

Like Alan, many other students made noticeable strides in their ability to concentrate. Brian entered my class unable to concentrate or focus his attention well. He wiggled around continually during centering times and spent most of his academic work time out of his seat or fiddling at his desk. At the same time he was very bright and performed very well on academic tasks when he did concentrate. One morning in January, Brian kept his eyes closed during the whole meditation for the first time. He looked like a miniature saint keeping his body so still. Afterwards he was very proud of himself for staying quiet the whole time. He went to his seat and focused on his math work quietly for the rest of the hour. This was unusual for him. He worked without having to be reminded to go back to his seat or to go back to work. He finished his five minute math drill for the first time in weeks. I was amazed, because I usually had to prod and prod to get him to complete his math drill. He then continued to work hard in his math folder. During the second hour of the morning I had to direct him into his reading work but, once directed, he worked *very hard* and got a lot done. During the third hour Brian lost his new-found concentration and did not get his cursive writing done, but it was good to see him concentrate well for the first time during a two hour block of academic learning time. During the rest of January, Brian continued to challenge himself in keeping his body still and eyes closed during most of the meditation times. Some days were harder than others for him. His desire to experience his new-found inner world was obvious in the way he now came quickly to the meditation rug, putting his pillow in a spot where no one would disturb him. In fact, when I questioned him about his new ability to concentrate he replied, "I'm not sitting next to anyone I might goof off with." He had become aware of the fact that to experience his inner world was so beautiful that he did not want to jeopardize the experience in any way. Brian had begun to enjoy the rich images which emerged during meditation, and his concentration continued to improve as his participation in meditation increased. He began to do good cursive writing work, and by the end of the year *his word recognition level was equal to that of an eighth-grader*, as shown in Rosebank's quick assessment tests.*

Brian's eyes began to sparkle with a warm glow. He seemed to have found a new source of joy and contentment. He enjoyed sharing his new-found images with the class. Here is one of them:

> I was a balloon and I had a fat friend. He was blowing me up and all the air was going out of him and I was as big as the universe and he was as skinny as a pencil.

Brian's mother shared with me that Brian did centering at home on his own, as well. She said, "He also told us several times how to do it. He even made a tape of himself leading it, which he named 'Instructions for Centering'. The whole family does centering with his tape sometimes. Brian does centering at night before going to bed, when he is afraid of the dark or lonesome or not feeling quite right. Because of centering he has become better able to handle inner and outer conflicts and better able to like himself. He has also become more reasonable and much less hyperactive."

Another parent noted the following change in her son as a result of his participating in meditation twice daily for one year: "Mainly he seems able to concentrate on things for a longer period of time. Also his quiet times are a little longer. Thank Heaven! He uses centering at bed time and he has no trouble going right to sleep."

Many parents seemed happy with the effects that meditation was having on their children, and I as a teacher was overjoyed with it. Compared with my earlier years of teaching, it seemed to be working miracles. As for the children themselves, Anthony summed up his feeling about meditation in the classroom one morning when he said, "If I ever become a teacher I'm going to have my class do centering." I asked, "How come, Anthony?" He responded, "Because it makes me feel *so good.*"

---

*Rosebank's quick assessment tests are a series of short tests designed to allow the teacher to assess quickly a child's progress in reading and math.

In the stillness.

CHAPTER 4

The Five Steps

Some people believe that meditation is some bizarre religious practice, and they fear it. But as I said before, it is really nothing more than just being still. This stillness, however, is not as easy as it sounds, and that is why the techniques of meditation have been evolved by people down through the centuries. The meditation I use with children includes five steps:

a. Getting in touch with and relaxing the body
b. Deep breathing to change and get control of emotions
c. Concentration of the mind
d. Expansion of the mind with imagination and intuition
e. And grounding the new-found high level awareness into a productive activity

These steps are outlined in Deborah Rozman's book, *Meditating With Children**. Children are able to tune to their inner wisdom much faster than adults are, because they do not have as many concepts built up in their minds as to how things should be or ought to be. Their minds are supple and flexible, not bogged down with thoughts about what happened yesterday or what is going to happen tomorrow. They live much more in the moment—in the now. With children, tuning to inner wisdom comes naturally, once the child has gained control over the body and mind. The challenge is getting them ready. How does one get thirty or forty wiggly, excited children all quiet with eyes closed at

---

*Deborah Rozman, *Meditating With Children*, (Boulder Creek, CA: University of the Trees Press, 1975).

the same time? I start the children with a first step of getting in touch with their bodies and relaxing them. Some stretching or yoga exercises are good for this. Young children love to pretend that they are animals as they do the different yoga postures. Rachel Carr's book *Be a Frog, A Bird, or a Tree** is excellent. The Rag Doll exercise from *Exploring Inner Space*** is also wonderful for getting in touch with the body and for relaxation. After yoga exercises I have the children tense and relax each body part, starting with the toes and ending with the top of the head. This can be done standing up or sitting down, eyes opened or closed, depending on the age of the children you are working with. Next I gather the children around the edges of a large circular rug. Each child has a pillow. I have the children sit crossed legged on the pillows, hands resting on their laps, palms upward. But you can also have your children sitting on chairs with feet flat on the floor, backs straight and not leaning against the chair back. It is very important to help the children learn to keep the back straight, as a crooked back blocks a natural flow of energy up and down the spine. It is now important to have the children close their eyes, if they have not already done so during tensing and relaxing. Closing the eyes blocks out the external stimulation of vision in order to tune into the inner world. I have the children tune quietly into what they are feeling—whether they are full of energy, joyful, sad, angry, or resentful. Any and all feelings are accepted. Deep breathing follows this step. The children breathe in to a count of 3 or 5 (depending on the age of the child), hold the breath to the same count, 3 or 5, and breathe out to a count of 3 or 5. As they breathe in, I have them imagine that fresh new life force and energy are entering their bodies with the breath and spreading throughout their bodies as they hold their breath. As they breathe out I have them imagine any negative feelings—sadness, boredom, anger, or tiredness—are coming out through their noses and leaving their bodies and disappearing. On the inbreath I may encourage them to breathe in love, joy, peace, or happiness piggyback along with the fresh energy and life force. This breathing step is a very powerful tool which enables children to change their emotions at will. In the classroom I have found that once children learn this step, they begin to use it whenever they are feeling

---

*Rachael Carr, *Be a Frog, a Bird, or a Tree* (New York: Doubleday, 1973).
**Christopher Hills and Deborah Rozman, *Exploring Inner Space, Awareness Games For All Ages* (Boulder Creek, CA: University of the Trees Press, 1978).

Stretching releases tension; this yoga posture is called the camel.

tired or upset. They begin to learn what it feels like to be calm and centered and to know that they can re-create that space any time they want to. They will often come in from recess and ask if they can go to the centering corner, if something has upset them while outside.

The third step is concentration. Concentration is focusing the mind in one point. I usually have the children concentrate on a point between their eyebrows. They concentrate on a star or visualize a candle flame in between the eyes for as long as they can, drawing all their energy and attention into that point while staying very relaxed. I encourage them to let any stray thoughts or memories pass through, always gently drawing the attention back to the star or candle flame.

Once the children's bodies, emotions, and minds are quiet, the children are ready for the fourth step: true meditation—that turning inside for their own answers and wisdom. At this point, the intuition and imagination are heightened. This is the time the child may have intuitive flashes or visions equal to those of poets, artists, and visionaries. At this point I usually help the children expand their imagination and awareness through guided imagery. We may take off in our imaginary spaceships and try to find the ends of the universe, or we may imagine we are a seed asleep in the moist warm earth and go through the stages of growth, culminating in a beautiful flower. Often in the morning I have the children use the focused, heightened state of awareness to meditate on the day ahead, using the creative imagination to aid them in doing better in their academic work, reading, math, spelling, etc. Many people think of the imagination as a world of unreality but in fact it is just the opposite. We actually create our reality with the thoughts and images which we hold in our minds. So in this step the children see themselves on a movie screen in their minds, reading well, doing math well, and spelling well. If the class has been having trouble with unkind behavior, such as name-calling, I may have them use their heightened awareness to tune into what true caring really is.

It is now time for the fifth step: grounding the new-found energy, wisdom, insights, and heightened awareness into some useful and productive activity. We do not want to leave children hanging at this point because they may get used to just living in the fanciful world of images and visions, never bringing them into concrete reality or expressing them so that others will understand them. So at this point I have the children get back in touch with their bodies by tensing their muscles and letting them go and then opening their eyes. As they look around, they simply shine with energy and quiet excitement. I direct them to channel this newly focused energy and creativity into dance, art, story writing, music, sharing, class discussions, creative communication, awareness games, or academic work. At this point the children love to express their new-found images verbally, in pictures, and in story writing. It all flows naturally from the child's heightened imagination. Problem solving becomes easy in this heightened state.

In teaching the children to meditate, you are teaching them self-discipline. The more a child is able to get control of the emotions, the mind, and the body, and tap that wonderful world of internal wisdom, images, and peace, the more rewarding meditation becomes for the child. He gains concentration and self-mastery and is able to deal much more effectively with the demands and pressures of his world of peers, teachers, sibling disturbances, etc. He gains a quiet, non-egotistical self-confidence, beautiful to observe. Being able to focus his mind, the child can do better in anything he chooses to do.

"Fill your body with fresh life force. Feel it bathing your cells."

CHAPTER 5

How to Start

I find it best to start meditation the very first thing the first day of school. Shortly after all the children have entered the classroom and have had a few minutes to adjust to their new environment, I ask them to come and sit around the edges of the rug. I explain to the children that we are going to do an exercise called "centering."* I stress that this is the most important thing we do because it prepares us for the rest of the day and helps us do better in all we are doing. I ask them to try their best and not disturb others around them.

I explain to the children that we are going to practice relaxing our bodies, getting in touch with our feelings, and imagining fresh energy coming into our bodies. I tell them we are going to go on an exciting journey in our imaginations. I say that this is a very special experience and if they try really hard they may experience some wonderful peaceful feelings inside or see beautiful pictures in their minds.

I find it best to keep the first meditation very short—two minutes maximum—so that it is an exciting, fun experience for the children. Since it takes much self-discipline for the child to learn to keep his eyes and body quiet for longer periods of time, I very slowly increase the

---

*If you are teaching in a conservative district, it is better to use the word "centering" rather than the word "meditation", since some people think that meditation is a religious practice. Centering is a good word, since what we are doing is relaxing and letting go, in order to discover the calm center within.

length of the meditations. In the first meditations I either leave out some of the steps or make the steps very short. For instance, instead of having the children tense and relax each body part, I may have them tense and relax their whole body at once, and do this two or three times. Or I may have the children tense and relax their body parts standing up with eyes open and only have them sit quietly with eyes closed for the next three steps: getting in touch with feelings, rhythmic breathing of fresh life force, and expanding the awareness with the imagination. I usually take the children on a journey in their imaginations the first time because they enjoy getting in touch with this part of themselves so much.

On the first morning of the first day I usually lead the children on a journey in their rocketships on and on into outer space. Afterwards we tense our bodies and open our eyes. Many children say, "Wow," as they open their eyes. Their eyes shine with energy and excitement, and many are smiling. They obviously really like it, and they love to

A journey through space.

share what they saw in their imaginations. Even though it was their first experience with centering, several of the children in the class where I first began to teach meditation saw tiny purple men in rocketships. One boy found himself in a meteor war. He saw an explosion first, then the meteors going in all directions. He directed his spaceship through the meteors. Some children took their rocketships through the sun. The exciting discussion brought us all closer together. The reason I have the children sit on a large rug in a circle is because I found it much more difficult to keep their attention when I had them sit in their own seats. When scattered about the room, they do not seem to relax as much or go as deep. In a circle it is easier to stay in touch with the children and to keep your rhythm and pace in tune with them. There is less chance of their energies being distracted when they are all focused into the center. Make sure everyone has enough room and that no one is touching. Some or all of the children will want to take their shoes off because it is more relaxing. It is best to have them leave their shoes near their desks because if they have them in front of themselves they tend to play with them during meditation. Nothing should be brought with them to meditation time.

As I mentioned in the previous chapter, I always encourage the children to keep their backs straight, often finding it best to remind them more than once to check their backs in a fun way during the five steps. For instance I may say, "Make sure you are ready to take off into outer space by checking your eyes, are they closed? Now check your back. Is it straight?" Almost instantly all backs are straightened and eyes are closed. It is vital that children work on the discipline of keeping their backs straight. Energy naturally flows up and down our backs when they are straight and this is enhanced naturally during meditations. A sloppy back inhibits this flow of vital force. It helps to have the children double-check themselves in this way throughout the whole meditation. Several times during the meditation I may say, "Double-check yourself, now. Are your palms up?" Lots of positive reinforcement helps, also, not directed to individuals, however, because that singles children out and can be embarrassing to them. For instance, I may say, "It's nice to have everyone ready to start," or "Everyone has been very still the whole time. Thank you for being so quiet." If you say this when one or two children are a bit restless they will usually then re-join the quiet vibration of the rest of the class.

Talk to the children in your most loving voice. Make it calm, smooth and relaxing. You can lead the children spontaneously or you may wish to start out by taping a few meditations and playing them for your class, or you can purchase a tape from the University of the Trees.* If you do so, you have the advantage of meditating along with your students and setting an example. As you already know, children often unconsciously and consciously model themselves after us. Maureen Murdock, a kindergarten teacher from St. Augustine in Florida, who wrote her Master's thesis on her experience teaching children to meditate, always keeps her eyes closed as she leads her class, knowing they will learn best through example. She found this worked very successfully with her kindergarten class. After the meditation her students would ask anyone who poked or disturbed them to not do so again. She found her students respected one another's wishes to have it quiet during meditation time.

I usually keep my eyes closed as I lead the class, but keep my ears very attuned to any restlessness or disturbance. At first there will always be a few who may disturb. If I hear restlessness I open my eyes to observe how the group is doing. In this way I can check and see who is having trouble keeping their eyes closed and body still. If I notice a child is having special problems, I take him aside later and discuss it with him. It is also good to take those who are having trouble and to work with them in small groups. Sometimes I have those who are having difficulty (especially hyperactive children) sit in a small circle within the larger circle of children. Putting an encouraging hand on the shoulder of a restless child often helps him to relax and enter into the meditation.

Most children will like meditation right from the start. A few will resist it because it is a discipline which requires self-control, something probably not demanded so far in their lives. Those who have much difficulty keeping their eyes and body still, will begin to like meditation as soon as they gain control. They start to discover wonderful feelings

---

*Two cassette tapes for children are available from the University of the Trees Press: "UNCLE ALF'S COSMIC CIRCUS" — A special mime/chant meditation with participation for small children and adult children. It is followed by meditations on the cuddly teddy bear, dreaming about sheep playing, an unusual animal chanting meditation, and meditation for peace and quiet, by Christopher Hills, and "MEDITATING WITH CHILDREN" — A selection of taped meditations from the book *Meditating With Children*, narrated by Deborah Rozman.

"Because it feels so good."

of calm within, the wonder of their own inner truth and imagination. They gain much self-confidence and are quite aware of their progress. I have found that at about 2:00 in the afternoon young children become tired and restless and you can't do much serious work with them. One afternoon at about 2:00 I led the class through a centering activity. Immediately afterwards I gave them a spelling test. My hopes proved true. Calm and refreshed, the children worked as quietly as they usually do first thing in the morning. Encouraged by this success I decided to apply centering to rainy days. The two worst times on a rainy day occur the last hour before lunch time and immediately following the lunch hour. I tried centering the children at these times. The children settled right down and became quite manageable.

I require all students to participate in meditation because I have found that only by doing it do they discover the benefits. If a child cannot keep his eyes closed the whole time, I ask him to look down at the floor or sit quietly and not disturb others. Most children will challenge themselves and try to keep themselves still for longer and longer periods of time. I take time to talk with and encourage those who continue to have difficulty.

I am very consistent about the type of behavior I expect from the children. Learning to discipline children during meditation has taught me how to maintain better control over a class in all other activities, from class discussions to small group lessons. My standards and expectations of children have increased because of this.

When starting to teach meditation to children, it is good to begin with a sense of conviction. I did not really know what I was doing when I first taught meditation to the children. I was going on pure faith. I did not meditate myself at the time and had only done a little meditation on my own a few years prior to that. But something about Deborah Rozman's vibration and sense of conviction convinced me. I was determined it was going to work with my students, and it did. And that is one of the most important ingredients for anyone who wants to teach meditation: you must have a sense of conviction.

Teaching meditation is not like teaching reading or math. You can teach those subjects in many different ways. But with meditation you are drawing the children into a vibration with you, you are creating a vibration together, you are working from the level of the heart. I can teach reading with my hands tied behind my back. But not meditation. If I allow myself to get one bit bored or routine or uninterested, the children too become bored or restless. In this sense meditation becomes a challenge to teach. You've got to constantly be aware of the vibration you are creating. Because I was not a meditator myself when I first started out teaching meditation, I did not experience what the children were experiencing. That is where the sense of conviction comes in. If you believe it will work, it will. The more you participate with the children the more you will experience what they are feeling. When people ask me what is the best way to learn to teach children to meditate, I always answer, "Meditate yourself." Over the past five years, I have gotten more and more into meditation myself. This has really helped me know and experience what I want the children to experience and helps me know how to communicate it to them, not only from a talking level, but on the level of setting the tone and vibration of the meditation. For instance, when I ask the children to breathe in fresh life force and energy from the cosmos, I imagine our whole circle is full of that fresh life force and energy. I send peace and energy from my own being and heart to the children. In fact, I don't feel integral to ask the children to get into that vibration if I do not get into it myself.

A great help to anyone starting to teach meditation is Deborah Rozman's book, *Meditating With Children*. You can be successful teaching meditation right from the start if you follow her guidelines closely because it is all laid out for you very clearly. All you need to add is your enthusiasm, excitement and sense of conviction. As you begin with the children you will discover that meditation can have an immediate effect on your class, even if you feel a bit shaky about it at first and are not too sure of yourself. Results will help build your confidence and you'll soon be glad you took the risk to try something very new!

Discovering herself.

CHAPTER 6

Helping Children
Who Have Difficulty

Some children like centering from the first day of school. Those are the children who look at you wide-eyed after their first centering experience and say, "That was great!" One such child was Joseph. He seemed to really enjoy centering and afterwards would share wonderful feelings from his meditations. One afternoon after a centering activity in which we imagined we were walking in a forest, he expressed with a wide grin, "Oh, does that feel good!" Other children take more time to really get into it. Brian didn't get into it until about mid-year, but after that, he could hardly wait to center each day.

Kids who tell you they don't like centering may be saying so because they aren't really participating in it yet. One of my children's fathers came in one morning during the second week of school, concerned because his son didn't want to come to school because he didn't like centering. If a child doesn't like centering, I usually have a talk with that child to find out why. I talked to the son that day, and he expressed that nothing was happening when he meditated and that it was boring. I suggested he really give it a try, really try to do all the steps and see if that made any difference. He agreed to try, and during that week he gave it all he had. He didn't open his eyes right after meditation, and he seemed to go deeper. One morning he expressed that he felt like he was floating during meditation. After that he often referred to feelings of peace following meditation. Once he began to try, he began to feel something from meditation and began to like it. As the year progressed he began to see a recurring image in his meditations. He described it as a ditch with different colors in it. I did not understand the image, so I asked a parent who worked with dreams to see if he could understand it. He suggested that I have the child draw what he was imaging. The drawing turned out to be a mandala with a red circle in the center and all the colors of the rainbow around it in concentric circles, the last circle being violet. He drew the mandala several times. It seemed to have deep meaning for him.

Bill, seven years old, had trouble keeping his eyes closed during centering, when he first entered the class. At first he did not see or feel anything, but two months later, he began to be able to concentrate more. He began to say, "I really see something in my imagination now," and he began to enjoy centering. Some children need time to get into it. They need lots of encouragement along the way. It is not important that the children see anything in their imaginations. Some never do. Encourage the children to *feel* the meditation, to feel the energy going in and out of their bodies as they do the rhythmic breathing, to feel the softness of a cloud or the sweetness of a flower. Use the five senses a lot in leading the children in meditation. For instance, in leading them in the water meditation from Dr. Rozman's book, *Meditating With Children*, have them feel the wetness and power of the wave; have them smell the mist and hear the crashing sounds.

The children will often want to share afterwards what they saw in their meditations. It is all right to have those who see images from their meditations share them if you also make a space for children who do not see images to share so that they, too, can express what they felt from the meditations. Never allow the children to feel that there is something wrong with them or that they are inferior because they cannot see anything in their imaginations.

When I first began to meditate four years ago I had a rich world of images to draw on, but I no longer see much in my imagination. Instead I feel feelings of deep peace and joy. It is not that I cannot see images but that I no longer have any desire to see them. I made the mistake one year of putting too much emphasis on images the children were sharing from their meditations. This caused a girl who could not see anything in meditation to feel frustrated, like something was wrong with her. It also caused the children to tell stories obviously made up, which had nothing to do with what we were meditating on. If the children begin to tell stories following meditation which are far removed from what the theme of meditation is, I stop having the children share after meditation for awhile and have them go straight into art or story writing. Sometimes I do this anyway because I want them to use all the rich feelings they experienced in the centering in their drawings. If they share first, some of the energy gets diffused.

The main purpose for having children meditate is to help them get in touch with their own center of peace. The imagination can help to find this space and that is why it is used as part of meditation. The imagination includes all our senses. Some children will smell more acutely in their imaginations, others will hear, see, touch, or taste more sensitively. That is why it is good to include all five senses, if you can, when you lead a meditation.

If children are having difficulty with their imagination and feel frustrated by it, I find it good to have them close their eyes and visualize their mothers. I might say to such a child, "Close your eyes and see your mother looking at you. Imagine she is giving you a hug. Smell how good she smells. She is gently stroking your hair. Now she tells you how much she loves you." Children who think their imagination is blocked usually find it open when they visualize their mothers. Often their imagination was not blocked in the first place, they just weren't aware they were using it all along. Mother is usually so close to their heart, it is easy for them to experience her in their imaginations.

Another thing which helps children who are not aware that they are able to visualize is to use the word "pretend" instead of the word "imagine". Instead of saying, "Imagine you are in your spaceship flying farther and farther out to the end of the universe," say, "Pretend you are in your spaceship." One little boy said, "When you said pretend, I could really see it!" I have found this also works very well with adults who doubt that they can visualize.

If a child is having trouble with meditation I find it best to work individually with that child. I always start with a one-to-one talk.

Children are not always in touch with what is bothering them but by talking to them you can often get a sense of what to do next. One little girl (age seven) was fidgeting around and keeping her eyes open during centering. She did not have a very good attitude towards centering. After talking it over with her I decided to invite her to meditate with me at lunch time. After eating her lunch, she arrived with a very excited look on her face. I suggested that she lead me in a meditation which she willingly did. It was a beautiful meditation full of sensitivity and love. I had not known she had so much sensitivity and caring inside, as she always presented a somewhat hard exterior to myself and the other children. I peeked at her a few times as she led me. She had her eyes closed the whole time, smiling sweetly. From then on she participated much more willingly and joyfully in meditation. That one little personal interaction really made a big difference for her.

Sometimes the children complain that the meditations are too long. This can be a sign that I am presenting them in a boring way. In fact, I find if I don't have my whole heart and being into leading a meditation, the children pick it up and open their eyes more and become more restless, especially those who are easily distracted. When this happens I find I have to really give myself a push to make the meditation more exciting. I make sure I am including all five senses. The children will then remark that the meditation seemed shorter. Actually it wasn't. The children were just more absorbed.

For a while, during the third year that I led the children in meditation, I became bored with leading it. I stopped putting as much energy into planning the meditations and began to repeat some of the same meditations over and over again in the same way. This was during the month of February. The children began to complain that they didn't want to meditate any more. Some of the children who were complaining had been enjoying meditation for a year and a half. It felt very bad to have turned them off to something they had been so enthusiastic about. I really had to confront myself for allowing myself to get so lax. When I made a change and became excited and enthusiastic about leading them, the children began to enjoy meditation again. Now I try to watch my state of consciousness. If I find I feel somewhat lethargic and not too excited about leading the class in meditation in the morning, I do something out of the ordinary such as make up a whole new meditation. I get playful. I weave in stories about

Well worth it.

my own childhood into the meditation. This of course lights up the children's enthusiasm.

Some children find it hard to sit still. If a child is an especially hyperactive or restless child, I often have him sit next to me and I rub his back gently as I lead the meditation. This really seems to help calm the child. He will express afterwards how much he appreciated it. I know a first-grade teacher who led meditation in her class by sitting in the center of the circle and touching the children softly whenever they became restless. She said it really helped the children learn to stay still.

Some children go in and out of being able to concentrate, doing well for a few months and not so well for the next few months. Children seem to have natural rhythms, just as we adults have. How many of us feel fired up and excited one month about teaching and not so enthusiastic the next? Sometimes a child loses concentration because something disturbing has happened at home. At these times centering can be very helpful, even though it may be harder to do. If a child begins to have trouble after doing well for awhile, work with him one-to-one.

As I said earlier, I set high standards of behavior for the children I work with because I know that if the children really challenge themselves, they will experience fulfillment. I have found it important, however, to balance these high standards with sensitivity to each child's ability. I had one student who always seemed to wiggle about during meditation. I continually encouraged him to try harder. Sometimes I felt annoyed with him because I thought he could do better. The school made a video tape of the children meditating, which we showed at a Children's Health Symposium. The child's mother saw her son meditating on the video and commented, "I don't think he has ever been so still in all his life." I realized that perhaps my expectations of the child were a bit too high. I became more tolerant of his restlessness after that, realizing he was doing his best.

At the end of one year I had a girl who began to get very restless during meditation and express that she didn't like it. Because I was so busy with other things, I did not have a one-to-one with her to try to work out her problem. As a result she left the class with a negative attitude towards meditation. In retrospect I don't feel good about this and wish I had worked more with her. At different times during the year it is important to check in with each child and see if they are still with you in meditation.

One parent shared with me that her son did not understand why he was doing it, at the beginning of the year, and this caused him to worry inside himself. She suggested that I explain more clearly to the children what the imagination was. In a one-to-one talk, the child can share with you what he does not understand or what may be bothering him. You can't assume that they are all enjoying it or are getting anything from it. They may not be. As I said earlier, towards the end of the year it is especially important to continue tuning in to the children.

Meditation is a discipline. As in painting, jogging or any other sport, we reach a plateau and need encouragement to go on. Because of this, children will not always want to do it and will sometimes say, "Do we really have to do centering today?" In my own life I can think of the times I have had to struggle to get myself to sit down and meditate, but once I did it, I would come away refreshed and fulfilled afterwards. It is the same for children. I have had a whole class complain and not want to do it, and then afterwards be very excited to share the feelings and images they got in touch with. For this reason I always talk in a positive way to the children about meditation. If they say, "Do we have to do it today?" I answer in a cheery voice, "Of course, we do it every day just like we do math or reading." I counter their complaints with positive energy. This is, of course, when I know they are just having trouble with the discipline of doing it. If their complaints are coming because I have made the meditations uninteresting, then I change the manner in which I am leading them. The main thing is—don't give up just because the kids complain. Discover the cause. Stay enthusiastic and positive. Help individuals who may be having troubles. Change whatever you need to change about the way you are leading them. It's all very much worth it in the end.

Meditation teaches the child wonderful concentration.

CHAPTER 7

The Administration and Parents Respond

One of the questions which nearly every teacher asks me who teaches in public school is how do you get past the administration? How do you avoid parent complaints?

If you are teaching in a conservative public school district, as I was, and you doubt whether people will accept the fact that you are teaching meditation in the class, don't call it meditation. Call it "relaxation and centering techniques". Make up some name of your own that you know will be accepted. You can call it "concentration and mind expansion exercises". Make up a name which will let the administration and parents know you are doing something really good for education. I was lucky to have my superintendent, Dr. Don Slezak, behind what I was doing. During my three years of teaching meditation in the Scotts Valley Public School System he continually supported and encouraged me.

My principal was a bit more dubious about my intention to teach meditation to children. During the first week I started using it in the classroom, I shared with him about what I was doing. He knew it was meditation, since he had heard Dr. Rozman speak at our "in-service" before school began. I was always very open with him about what I did in the classroom. Because of this he trusted me and usually let me try out new things if I had a good reason behind what I was doing. He seemed relieved as I explained to him it was non-religious and exactly how I was doing it. Later on, as he began to see and hear about the wonderful effects meditation was having on my students, especially from parents of children in my class, he began to become enthusiastic and supportive. The same day I started using meditation in the classroom, another teacher at another school in our district, Vine Hill School, also decided to try it. I called it centering. She called it meditation. The next day five or six parents called her principal complaining that she was teaching meditation, which they considered religious. Her principal asked her to stop. That is why, if you plan to begin to teach meditation in your school, you may wish to give it another name. Scotts Valley is a very conservative school district with many people with traditional and fundamentalist religious beliefs. The word "meditation" upset them at Vine Hill School because they didn't know what it really was. You have to tune-in and see what is really best for your own situation.

Actually, the parents of children in the class can be the greatest asset in getting the administration behind what you are doing. The parents are the people you want to communicate with. Once they see the real benefits and effects meditation is having on their children they become very supportive. During the first year that I taught meditation to children, whenever parents came in and asked me about centering, I would always sit down with them and explain the process, all the steps I was using. I shared with them how the children had become more calm and caring in the classroom. I showed how increases in children's ability to concentrate had affected their academic work. This usually really excited the parents. I would then discuss how children and adults both have so little time in our society to relax or find any sort of inner calm or peace in a busy day, and how the centering helped children find this.

Every year that I taught, I always took slides of the children which I showed at Back to School Night in October and at Open House in April. On Back to School Night all the teachers were required to give the parents of children in their class an overview of the curriculum for that year. Open House was a night to come and see displays of the children's work, collected throughout the school year. Since I did not like standing in front of the parents, giving what seemed to me to be a dry discussion of curriculum every October, I began to take slides of the kids, and as I showed them, I was able to give the parents a good overview of the school year. The first year teaching meditation I showed slides of the children doing meditation, along with other pictures from the school year. I explained the process and told the wonderful results I had had with it during the year. The parents were very open and excited about what I shared. Some came up afterwards and expressed their appreciation that their children were able to get something like this in school.

At different times during the year different parents dropped by to express their feelings about the centering process. One bright warm May afternoon Phil's mother came to visit. She said, "I'm so glad the kids are doing centering. Phil does it now every time he plays soccer. It's a very private experience to him and he gets angry if I interrupt him. Every child in our family gets five minutes uninterrupted time at dinner to discuss his day. Phil often talks about centering at this time. He tells how it helps him concentrate better in his work. He is very serious about it." Phil was a very quiet boy with quite a temper once it got going. It was good to hear how much centering meant to him.

Sandy's mother became very excited about the centering when she first heard about it at Back to School Night. She said she wished centering had been taught by her teachers when she was young. She expressed, "I sincerely hope more teachers become interested in your approach. I wish my son could have had the same thing." About Sandy she said, "Sometimes Sandy will center while we are in the car or in her room when she feels tired. When she does this, she seems more refreshed. I have noticed an increased creativity in her story telling and writing, and her drawings and paintings."

The parents who worked in the classroom as aides and had the opportunity to actually observe the children centering and to see the results afterwards, became the most supportive of the process. Unfortunately, when I taught in public school, I felt too nervous to have the parents actually participate in the process with us, unless they asked to, not because I was uptight about the process itself, but because I felt too self-conscious to have parents watch me teach *anything*. Therefore, I usually would have parents like Alice, who volunteered in the classroom, work quietly in a nearby part of the room while I led the class in centering. If I were still teaching in public school I would now have the parents participate with the children. In the private school where I now teach I ask every guest who visits the classroom to participate in the meditation with us. They really appreciate being able to participate and come away knowing from within themselves why the process is good for the children. As one guest expressed, "No wonder you have them draw and write stories afterwards! I saw some beautiful images in my imagination. What a great way to teach!" But, as I say, I was much more conservative in the public school. So as it happened one morning, Alice, a parent aide, came to help in the classroom. She worked quietly correcting math booklets in a corner of the room as I led the children through centering. We did a usual meditation with relaxation, breathing, concentration on a star, and focusing on having a good day. We breathed in good feelings and breathed out upset feelings. Afterwards Roger, Alice's son, said that his hamster had died that morning and that he felt better now after centering. Alice came up at recess time and told me how glad she was that Roger had centered. Her eyes were moist with tears. She explained that Roger had been quite shaken before school that morning and the centering had really helped him get into a better space.

Alice became very supportive of the centering in the classroom. We had many discussions about Roger and how he was growing. She shared the following towards the end of the year: "Roger likes centering and uses it at home sometimes, too. If he has a difficult job to do (like cleaning a very messy room) he will sometimes center on getting it all done. Before we left on vacation he said he centered on getting along with Ruthie in the car so they wouldn't fight." She said, "I like centering in the classroom because it seems a good way to focus on the work and play of the day and to look inside oneself for peace and relaxation."

There were a few times that parents came in asking if they could participate in centering. Although I was nervous about it, I allowed them to stay and join us, if they asked. Sue, Eugene's mother, asked one day if she and her youngest son could stay for centering. So when I gathered the class into a circle I invited her and her son to join us. I led the children through a typical centering process. At the end I asked them to get in touch with how special it is to be alive, asking them to think of one thing they could do that day to love themselves or be kind to themselves. After centering was over, Sue sat for a few moments in wide-eyed calmness and then spoke softly, "That was great. Thank you." She seemed to be touched deeply somewhere in her being.

I suggest that you allow and encourage parents who visit or help out in the classroom to participate with you and the children in centering. Everyone who has participated in meditation with us in the private school where I now teach falls in love with it, including the Santa Cruz county superintendent of schools who visited our school this year. Everyone likes to get in touch with a sense of peace and calm within themselves. A lawyer who participated with us expressed afterwards that he wishes he started every day from the state of mind he got in touch with in the centering. One of the parent volunteers loved to come help out because she loved to center with us as the day began. Nothing will open the parents in your classroom more to the process of centering than participating in it themselves. I suggest that you lead your children's parents in centering at Back to School Night or at Open House. Afterwards, have them turn to the person sitting next to them and share what they saw or felt from the centering. We do this in workshops where we teach teachers and parents how to teach children to center and meditate. The centering followed by a brief sharing seems to really build a bond of closeness and trust amongst the participants.

Once the parents of the children in your class begin to see what's happening to their children because of centering, they will begin to tell your principal and superintendent about it. My principal began to tell me how pleased some of the parents were that I was teaching centering to the children. By the end of the first year I taught it, he had become very supportive of what I was doing. He wrote in my evaluation at the end of the 1976–77 school year: "(Stephanie) has effectively limited discipline problems by teaching her class the art of centering."

You will need to tune in and decide how it will be best to begin teaching centering in your school district. What happened to me, may or may not happen to you. Your sense of conviction will be of utmost importance to you. If you believe in yourself and what you are doing, others will too. Always share the wonderful results which I'm certain will occur in the students. Start low key. You may even want to start with just one of the steps of centering, perhaps the tensing and relaxing. Add more steps as you see it is being accepted by the children, parents, and administration. Take a risk! Be courageous. Try something totally new with children.

To close this chapter I would like to share Rema Stone's experience with her daughter Heather. Rema is a small motherly woman with warm eyes which twinkle when she smiles. Heather is a delicate, sensitive child with big brown eyes and a tendency to smile. Rema invited me out to lunch one afternoon, several years after Heather had been in my class. Over lunch she shared how centering had been one of the first positive things which helped Heather. She said Heather still did centering a lot at home. One afternoon while Heather was still in my class, Rema had come home from work upset, and seven-year-old Heather had led her in relaxation and centering. From then on they began to do it regularly together. Rema's face glowed as she shared how centering had become a part of their lives. I asked her to write down the changes she saw in Heather due to centering. She wrote:

> "At the end of the first-grade Heather was almost a nervous wreck. I had considered a family counseling program, but just couldn't convince myself of it. She was passed to second-grade with, 'We'll let her second-grade teacher worry about it.' I knew she was smart enough, but she would just cry and say, 'It's too hard!' and do no more than she had to. Later I found her problem was she was being yelled at too much, both at home and at school.
>
> "Not long into second-grade she came to me with a suggestion that I might try 'centering' (I had been yelling again). I was curious as to what she was talking about, so that night we had quite a long talk all about what 'centering' is. It was new to her and even newer to me. After trying it a few times, we began using it regularly.
>
> "Heather started changing not long after that. So did I. We 'centered' almost every night before going to sleep and whenever we had aches and pains of all sorts. Her attitude about school changed a lot. Her work started improving, she tried harder and enjoyed pleasing her teacher, who by this time had become the second most important person in her life, outside her

family. She hardly ever cried over 'too-hard' work or
threw temper tantrums because she couldn't do it.
When she started to get upset at home we would tell her
to 'center.' Perhaps we over-used it, after a while she
would say 'No!' but almost always she would gain control
again in just a little while, as if the suggestion or thinking
about it for a moment could make it happen.

"Here it is two years later. We also used centering
when we practiced childbirth at home (we called it
relaxation exercises at class). Since then we have worked
on our positive attitudes, what we CAN do well. Heather
is now a confident fourth-grader."

Rema Stone
Sept. 27, 1978

"It doesn't mean she's your girl friend just 'cause you care about her."

CHAPTER 8

The Joy of Caring

As I watched meditation changing the children, I realized that I could have the same peace. I was always a very loving teacher, but I didn't always have peace. I was often worried about what the principal and parents were thinking. I was almost never completely sure of myself. In fact, I had constant anxiety not just about school but about everything. But when I started leading the children in meditation, I began to feel some peace. So I decided to meditate for about five minutes right before the children came to school. I would go into my classroom, keep the lights off, and lock the door, sit down, close my eyes and relax all my body parts. I often imagined that a golden waterfall of love was flowing down from above, through the top of my head down into my heart, then out from my heart into the whole classroom. I would imagine that the students were there in the classroom and that my love was reaching out to them. I imaged I was breathing in love and breathing out love. As I did this exercise I began to feel a warm glow in my heart which gave me an inner strength that lasted throughout the morning. During the morning whenever I began to feel upset or scattered I would tune back into the waterfall of peace flowing down on me and would instantly feel an inner stillness. I found I could do this with my eyes open as I walked around and worked with the children.

Due to the children's growing sense of inner peace and my own, I began to trust the peaceful atmosphere in the classroom and could relax in it. During all the years that I had taught before, I had always had a nervous feeling in my stomach as I was teaching, wondering when the lid was going to blow, almost waiting for the next discipline problem to arise, expecting it. I had never been able to truly relax in my classroom. Now for the first time, once I began this meditation practice, I could really relax. It felt wonderful.

I began to meditate five minutes at lunch time and sometimes right after school, with door locked and lights turned out, to avoid being disturbed by children and other teachers. I found immediately I had more energy, enthusiasm, and inner peace. The meditation felt like taking an energy bath. I felt so refreshed afterwards. I no longer was drained in the afternoon, unless of course I skipped all exercises. Any time I needed to center myself I did, and found the children calmer and more self-directed as a result of my own calm.

I have discovered that children pick up my state of mind and being and send the energy back to me. Children are very intuitive by nature. They absorb what we are feeling and thinking unconsciously. Have you ever been about to say something and a student speaks up with exactly what you were going to say? It has always amazed me how my students know instantly in the morning how I am feeling. And they are so blunt in their evaluation, "You look tired," "Why are you so grumpy?" "You look pretty today." Children unconsciously pick up our vibrations, our moods and feelings, and send them back to us. I have found that to the extent that I allow myself to become uncentered, anxious, or scattered, the children begin to become anxious and noisy, too. They pick up my energy, and send it back like a mirror. Then I become ever so much more uncentered and it all snowballs. So it was well worth the extra few minutes before school and at lunch time to center myself, and I was now able to maintain a calm, pleasant atmosphere in the classroom. There were other benefits as well.

I have often had the feeling, as you undoubtedly have, of just too much to do: report cards, record keeping, lessons, correcting papers, getting activity centers ready, meetings. After trying meditation myself for about five months, I suddenly no longer had to work so many weekends and evenings. I had become more efficient—lifted out of being scattered to a level of seeing more clearly how I could do the same things in half the time. I also found intuitive ideas flowed to me in my meditations, such as what activity centers I should do for the week. My job became easier as ideas seemed to just flow through me.

A few times some of the children meditated with me in the mornings before school started. They were waiting outside my door when I arrived. I invited these children to come in and center with me. These were the best meditations! I felt a special closeness between their beings and my being at these times.

Now I try to meditate at least one half hour every morning before I leave my home and every afternoon before supper. I find if I skip it in the morning, I just don't have as much energy and bounce during the day. In the evening I find it very relaxing to tune back into a deeper part of myself, and I often feel refreshed enough to be able to go ahead and do some other activity. It's wonderful not to need as much sleep!

The more I began to use meditation in my classroom and to meditate myself, a wonderful thing happened: a caring, loving atmosphere evolved almost like magic. You could feel the love energy flowing from child to child. It was like a sweetness, as if the classroom flowed and hummed. We became more like a family than like a class; the children were becoming almost like brothers and sisters. It was a nice feeling, like the class was a happy space to be in. The children were eager to arrive in the morning and there were lots of smiles and laughter. They began to walk arm in arm, and you could see that they loved each other. I think that partly what had happened was that, through meditation, the children became more aware and sensitive, more able to sense another student's inner world. The children became more in touch with themselves and didn't have the need to express themselves in a negative physical manner. They began to care less about who was first in line or who was winning, even though children of this age normally want to be first for everything. Their egos found creative outlets for expression and no longer had such a drive and demand for constant recognition.

Eight-year-old Jeremy had problems with fighting during recess, often remaining angry for a full hour afterwards, unable to get any work done. After meditating daily for a month, he began to deal with his problem in a new way. He began to recognize what was happening inside himself. He would get angry but was able to watch himself get angry and then let it go. I watched him begin to gain control over his emotions, avoiding many potential fights. He was able to get in touch with his own inner power to control himself in an anxiety-producing situation. The following year, Jeremy's teacher reported to me that he blossomed into a model student.

Before I started using the centering exercises, I maintained the type of discipline where the children suffered consequences if they disobeyed one of the rules in the classroom. For instance, if children kept shouting out at me and would not allow me to speak to the group, the consequence would be to have them pick up litter around the yard at recess time. About one week after I started using centering, I realized I wasn't having anyone pick up papers anymore. Not only did I see the children become more caring, thoughtful, and disciplined in the classroom but I observed wonderful changes in their behavior on the playground. After I had been using meditation about one month, the boys and girls began to play together more. In the mornings a large group of my boys and girls began to congregate on the playground to have discussions. Usually children just wander around by themselves in the morning, a few boys playing over here and a few girls over there—definitely not together. When I first noticed the boys and girls talking together in a circle, I thought, "Wow, what's happening to my kids? They are really beginning to see each other in a different way." I feel this happened because the children were tuning into their inner feelings every day, and some of the blocks that children have—such as the attitude, "I'm not going to have anything to do with that person", began to disappear. It all happened spontaneously, in a way they weren't even aware of. They began to have more feeling for one another, so they just naturally began to relate more. The "I don't like boys" or "I don't like girls" attitude which had always been prevalent in my primary classes over the past seven years and which discussion could not eradicate was also disappearing. This change of consciousness was gradual but quite apparent, not only to myself but to others.

I began to notice other changes on the playground. Formerly, before the students participated in meditation, some of my boys were running around together causing problems, disturbing other students and walking past windows disturbing other classrooms. Several teachers were annoyed by this, and I found I was having to put a lot of energy into keeping tabs on these boys. A few months after practicing meditation in the class, these seven- and eight-year-old boys began to spontaneously organize themselves into sports. They started playing games such as soccer and football, and did this entirely on their own.

They organized, refereed, and played the games *by themselves*. They chose one person to be the referee and respected this referee. If he said, "Danny hit the ball out of bounds," then that was it, he hit the ball out of bounds. Everybody respected his decision. I was surprised at this development because I usually find children of this age very dependent on the teacher for decisions, and even when the teacher says, "Danny hit the ball out of bounds," the losing side will often argue. In previous years I had tried to organize competitive games (such as kickball) with my second- and third-grade students, but due to their constant bickering and fighting, I had given up, discouraged, though non-competitive games worked well with this age group. I discussed this problem with other teachers teaching the same grade levels and discovered most had experienced similar problems. Based on their experience and my own I decided that seven- and eight-year-olds were too immature emotionally to handle organized competitive games. But now with the new attitude in the children, I began to encourage the boys and girls who were interested, to play soccer, football, and baseball at P.E. time. I helped organize the teams but they played and refereed the games without my help, proud to play in front of me. P.E. became one of the most relaxing and enjoyable times of the day.

Visitors to my class often commented on the sense of caring my students showed to one another. The members of the California Monitor and Review Team, a group of people who evaluated our Early Childhood Program in January of 1977, commended me for the degree of care my students showed for one another and for their ability to take responsibility for themselves. Our school, Brook Knoll, was awarded the highest scores ever given a first-year school in the program. Since the team was looking for self-directed students in a loving atmosphere, I feel meditation helped us obtain the scores.

The next school year, 1977–1978, at the request of my principal, I taught a straight second grade, as opposed to a combination second-third grade class as I had taught the two previous years. Not long after

They organized, refereed, and played the games by themselves.

using meditation in this second-grade class, I again noticed the children becoming very sensitive and caring towards one another. Boys and girls, in a manner similar to that in the previous years, began to play together more than they had in any typical classroom I had taught before. They began to sit next to one another more easily during group activities. The boys began to invite some of the girls to their birthday parties. Boys and girls played together at recess time. During a "love circle" exercise* in which the children give feedback to one another, some girls said to a boy and vice versa, "You're a good friend to have." The boys expressed kindly to girls they didn't even relate to that much. In previous years when I was not teaching meditation, boys would not say much about girls and vice versa unless it was something silly or not nice.

---

*The "love circle" exercise is an awareness game from the book *Exploring Inner Space*. Awareness games are discussed in more detail in chapter 14.

One afternoon after a meditation in which I asked the children to think of one person in the room they could care more about and what they could do to show it, Joseph shared that he was going to care more about Laura by helping her get on the bars. He explained, "It doesn't mean she's your girl friend just 'cause you care about her."

On another morning Ellen shared a story about the night she stayed over at Roger's house: "We couldn't go to sleep and Roger and I kept on talking. Then we relaxed our heads, our eyes, our cheeks and everything. We imagined we were floating on a cloud. Then we shared our ideas. I told Roger I imagined I was an angel floating on a cloud. We went to sleep right away. When we woke up we did centering again. I imagined I could float anywhere I wanted. Then we got up."

I was surprised to hear Ellen had spent the night at Roger's house. In previous years boys and girls had not allowed themselves to become close enough to want to spend that much time with one another. At a later time Roger shared that he and Ellen liked to go over to one another's houses. He said they liked to tell stories and then do centering and experience the stories they made up in their minds. It warmed my heart to see how much they were enjoying doing meditation on their own.

Parents of the children in that class came to visit from time to time. Some shared how their children had become more thoughtful and caring since school started. Eight-year-old Tim's mother came in all smiles one morning. "Tim has become such a lover since being in your class," she said, "he gave me half a dozen roses the other day. He and Don bought a bunch of roses together. Tim gave me half and Don gave half to his mother. Tim gave his dad a rose when he was sick. He seems really mature for his age to be reaching out like that." Tim's mother felt the centering had helped him discover this part of himself.

Jeannie, another eight-year-old student, spoke up after centering one morning to tell how her mother had come home tired and that she and her brother laid a blanket on their mom. They closed the door to the kitchen, cleaned the kitchen up and set the table.

Another parent observed the following in her son after he had participated in meditation for two years: "I think he has become a much more sensitive, thoughtful, kind and caring person. I'm surprised at how aware he is of children's injustices to each other."

An especially heartwarming experience happened one afternoon when Dave's mother dropped by to talk with me after school. She talked about some difficulty she was having with her husband. As she was expressing herself her son walked in, overhearing our conversation. He said, "Mom, the trouble with you is that you don't center yourself." She asked him to show her how which he did BEAUTIFULLY, and a wonderful communication happened then between the three of us. I had not known that the meditations had affected Dave so much since he had always seemed somewhat resistant to them.

I noticed the children became more caring towards me also. In late September they surprised me one morning. I asked them to come to the rug and get ready for centering. They all gathered around the bright blue rug I had purchased from a neighbor especially for meditation. Just then my aide Tanya walked in. I called her over and asked her to make a birthday card for Sonya whose birthday it was. My head was turned from the children as I talked to Tanya. When I turned around, to my surprise almost all 29 children had their eyes closed! I was tickled pink and expressed my appreciation. From then on the children were often ready for centering before I asked them to get ready. It was such a treat.

Other professionals noticed the increased caring among my students. Tony LaBue, our counselor, often visited my classroom because he liked to share in the loving atmosphere. He commented:

"One of the most significant changes I observed in
Ms. Herzog's class was the calm flow of energy among
the children. I was aware that the children were more
in charge of themselves and not in the process of using
the teacher's controls to accomplish their assignments
or to correct their behavior. The class atmosphere
had two distinct qualities: (1) a gentle flow of concern
for one another, and (2) a maintenance of controlled
excitement and enjoyment for their existence in the
classroom. This observation is based on the majority

*of students regardless of who was instructing the class.
The students did not exercise the testing and disorder
that is frequently found when a substitute teacher is
present. It is also important to note that Ms. Herzog's
control of her own energies, and not the children's,
aided tremendously in the balanced classroom
environment."*

Since I had begun meditating before school and at lunch times, I
was much more able to consciously stay calm and focused during the
school day, no matter what challenges arose in working with the
children. I soon discovered I could quickly bring myself to a state of
calm and maintain that state even in stressful situations.

Prior to teaching meditation, I found that whenever I was speaking, some children would not be listening. As all parents and teachers
well know, it is always a struggle to get everyone listening at the same
time. After I started using meditation the first year, I began to notice
long moments when all of the children were quiet the whole time I was
speaking; they were so attentive, their eyes would be right on me. I
began talking more to their inner beings—it kind of flowed naturally. I
began to relate more from the feelings in my heart, something that's
usually hard to do in a classroom. I felt as if they were actually hearing
me from deep inside.

There was a marked difference in the children's ability to listen and
follow directions in the first several weeks after participating in
centering activities. Because many children became very peaceful
after meditating, they were better able to take turns and really listen to
one another. At the end of the school year the children's scores in the
listening tests went way up. For example, one boy's score rose from
1.4 to 8.0 as recorded on the Stanford Achievement Tests.

The children's ability to be more self-directed and self-disciplined
allowed me to become more myself with the children and experience
more fulfillment than I had ever felt before in teaching. In September
of 1977 I wrote in my journal, "I am noticing a special joy among
myself and the children as we go through our day together. When we
sing I find I am less self-conscious, I am really getting into the beat of
the songs we sing and the children are really with me in spirit; smiling,

singing, and swaying their bodies. It's such a joy."

The special bond that I felt growing between myself and the children is best described in the following excerpt from my journal. The entry was written the first day back from Christmas vacation: "Today was the first day back to school. I felt anxiety about being back, not quite sure of how I would relate to the children and they would relate to me. The children responded very well to centering. They got ready quickly and kept their eyes closed the whole time. They seemed to be really happy doing it again. The thing that spoke most to my heart today, though, was that even though we have been separated for two weeks, there is still a special bond between myself and the children; it is a special bond of love that I cannot find words to express, I just kind of feel it or intuit it, and the children seem eager and happy to be back into school tasks. Many children walked arm and arm during the day. There is a kind of magic in my classroom and I love it."

Good friends.

The children and I had fallen in love with one another. We had all become more sensitive to one another's beings. This feeling of love grew deeper as the year progressed. On June 13, 1978, the day before school was out, we did our last centering meditation of the school year. We all knew it was the last. The children were very quiet and responsive. Afterwards, in the stillness, we sent love and energy around the circle, holding hands. A magical love pervaded the room, and I could feel the love and energy in my hands. It was quite powerful.

On the last day, as usual, a movie was shown to all the children in the school. After it was over the class walked with me back to the classroom. We walked hand in hand. Anna held onto my pants as she tugged along behind me. After a snack of cupcakes it was time to say good-bye. Many children came up to hug and kiss me. Roger really gave me a big hug. I experienced his quiet but penetrating love. It was hard for us to leave one another.

The next school year on the first day of school a throng of noisy excited children was crowded around the door to my classroom when I arrived. As I drew closer I thought, "Boy, this new class of students is sure eager for school to start." To my surprise I discovered they were the class from the year before. With excitement and joy and a few tears we greeted one another. We had only a few brief minutes to reunite in the heart before it was time for me to get ready for my new class and for them to look for their new classrooms.

Many times during the year, the children from that class, boys and girls alike, came to visit me at lunch time. They found all kinds of excuses to come over to the primary side of the building. It was always a joy to see them and they often stayed to help me get ready for the next class session. We had many warm sharings during these times. They always filled my heart with joy at being a teacher. The bond between us had stayed strong.

After teaching meditation for those two years, during the 1976–1977 school year and the 1977–1978 school year with wonderful results and changes in my students, I began to wonder, "What would happen to a classroom of hard-to-handle students if the teacher taught them meditation?" I had had just such a class in 1973–1974, three years before I started teaching meditation to children. That was my first year teaching at Brook Knoll School. As often happens the first year a person teaches in a new school district, I found myself landed with the worst behavioral problems in the second-grade class. (There were three second-grade classes and the most difficult kids to handle were in my class.) That year I had a student who threw desks over on his way into the classroom from the playground, expressing all the pain and frustration he felt in being separated from his father in a recent divorce. I also had Ron, a boy who had sudden uncontrollable fits right in the middle of a lesson, writhing and screaming in the middle of the room. These fits seemed to come on without any notice and were not triggered by any particular incident. The child would simply go into a state in which he was out of control of himself. He had been tested by psychologists and doctors who said it was a neurological problem. They said he would outgrow it as he grew older. That was no comfort to me, however, because I *had* him, and he certainly hadn't grown out of it yet. No one, including the school psychologists, knew how to help me. In fact, the boy's mother told me one day, "You just have to expect years like this when you're a teacher." (It's a wonder I didn't give up the profession right then and there.)

Many of the children in that same class were the products of divorces and were experiencing a lot of anger and hurt. I asked for help about midway into the year. Our counselor was able to spend some time with the children but not enough to really lighten the load. It was a difficult year and it had kindled even deeper the fire in my heart to search for a way to deal with discipline without being punitive or negative.

Later on, after I had successfully used meditation for two years, I looked back to that first year and thought, "What would meditation have done to a class like that?" It seems as if some higher power heard my thoughts because during the 1978-1979 school year, I again found myself in just such a classroom. Broken homes, sexual abuse and being left alone without parent supervision were all part of the lives of many children in my new classroom. They often took their frustrations out on me and on one another. Almost daily fights occurred on the playground between some of the children in the class. It was not uncommon to be faced with a group of crying, angry children after lunch. This is not to say that all the children in the class were like this, but there were enough disturbed children in the class to make it a more difficult class to teach. Now I had a chance to see if meditation could calm disruptive, hard-to-handle students. From the beginning of the school year this group of children responded well to meditation. I had had about half the students the previous year, and the old students set a good precedent for the new students. They already knew how to meditate and became leaders in creating a positive attitude towards meditation.

In leading this new class in meditation, I emphasized changing negative feelings to positive ones. I did this because the children seemed to have a great need to let go of pent-up feelings, and I felt inspired to help them in creating positive thoughts as counterwaves. After having the children tense and relax their bodies and then go inside to get in touch with feelings, I would say, "Breathe in the fresh new energy, feel it come in and fill up your whole body. Now let it go, sending away any angry or unhappy thoughts. Send them to the end of the universe and make them disappear there." After doing this two or three times I would have them draw in love with the energy on the inbreath and send out love and energy on the outbreath and share it with everyone in the meditation circle. Sometimes I would continue with a visualization such as this: "Now see yourself in your imagination on a movie screen in your forehead. See yourself just as you look today. See yourself having a wonderful day, doing your best in reading, math, and everything you do. See yourself caring for everyone in the class today."

On the first day of school that year, I led these children in a meditation during the first twenty minutes of the school day. I explained to the children how we would do centering every day and how important it was. Bertha, my classroom aide, shared with the children that first morning how her mind exercises helped her every morning to change her feelings. (Her mind exercises were a form of meditation she had used to heal herself of cancer and was continuing to use to stay healthy.) She told the children that her own children could tell when she had done her exercises in the morning because she was more caring towards them and they could really notice the difference. She explained to the class how her mind exercises were similar to the centering I was going to be leading them in every morning and how they could also observe how it would make them feel different. Every morning after that, the students would tune into Bertha, and tell her if she had done her mind exercises or not. The children could always tell.

In spite of all their problems, the disruptive children in the class seemed to like meditation from the very start. Perhaps this was because it offered a few minutes of inner peace and solitude, something they yearned for but didn't know how to get. Perhaps it was the only time these children had that peace. One especially disturbed boy often told long and beautiful stories to the class following meditation. Some of the girls who had ongoing conflicts and fights would often in their meditations spontaneously send love to those they had the greatest difficulty getting along with.

As part of the meditation one morning in October, I read the children a story by Norah Hills called *The Happy Spark* which is about a little spark some children found on the beach. The children in the story discovered that the little spark brought love and caring to anyone who needed it. Norah wanted to see how a group of children would respond to the story. The class loved it and began to bring images from the story into their meditations. Because of their positive response to the story, I began to lead the children in meditations which included the image of a star which spread its love out to the whole world and beyond, an image which I hoped would help foster a sense of caring, as the story of the star had. During these meditations the children often got in touch with beautiful (and sometimes humorous) images of reaching out and caring more for each other and for the whole world.

One afternoon after lunch I had the children imagine and focus on a small star inside their foreheads. They imagined their star shone brighter and brighter until it shone on the town of Scotts Valley, then on the whole world, and finally on the whole universe. Each time they put more love and energy into their star it expanded further and further into space, shining on all the other stars. At the end of the meditation they sent their star to shine on someone they loved.

Here are some of the children's images and feelings following their meditation.

Brian—"My star was as big as the whole universe and I shined it on everyone. It made all the criminals and bad people happy, all the good people happier, all the other people on other planets happy and robots and Martians and little bugs happy."

Sandy—"I sent some love to my family and the whole class, and a little more to Danielle because I really like her and I don't want her to leave." (At the end of the year Danielle was going back to live with her aunt in New York.)

Danielle—"My star was as big as the universe. These bugs came out. They told me my light was too bright so I made it smaller. Everybody was sad so I made it big and everyone was happy again."

Alan—"My star got bigger and turned into a starship. Then I saw the planet Mars and I fired my energy ray gun and the whole planet was happy and all the little green men were dancing around."

On Valentine's day that year I did a meditation which is one of the children's favorites. I had the children relax and imagine they were a special heart which grew larger and larger as they put more love into it until it included the whole universe. Stewart said afterwards, "I was God with a big heart and sent all the people love." Sandy said, "My heart was a big monster and it had these other little hearts inside and every time he would blow out these hearts, it would make everyone happy." Bill said, "When my heart-shaped balloon was growing, I took a giant arrow and I shot right through it and it squirted some love everywhere." Alan spoke next, "I sent little heart-shaped warm fuzzies filled with love to everybody in the classroom." Shawn shared, "When you said, 'tense your feet' I felt really good because your feet do a lot of stuff. And when you said 'blow up your heart balloon,' I blew it up and it was as big as the universe and it had the butterflies and all the horses—white and black horses—in it and it had all the bees and all the bugs and all the fishes in it and the universe was loving, too. To read this, you would never realize that Shawn was a very disturbed child. It touched my heart to see some of these children express such beautiful images, especially knowing how difficult it was for them to reach out of their own anger and hurt to care for another.

In spite of these meditations which emphasized changing negative feelings to positive ones and sending positive and caring energy out to the whole universe, changes in the new students' behavior and in the way they treated one another occurred slowly. Whereas in the previous two years a peaceful, loving atmosphere developed in the classroom in about one month, with this more difficult class it took much longer. During the first month I often went home exhausted from what it took to deal with the children's fights, name calling, and temper tantrums. The children in the class whom I had had the year before proved to be more self-directed than the new students. They often got annoyed when the new students caused trouble or didn't get ready for the classroom activities quickly.

One thing which I feel affected the new students' progress was the addition of a student teacher to the classroom. He was very skeptical about meditation and the awareness work I was doing with the children, and I allowed his critical attitude to affect me to some extent. Even though I was not always consciously aware of the tension this caused in me, in retrospect I can see that I was quite tense. Students always mirror how we teachers are feeling inside ourselves, and the children picked up my tension, became tense themselves and sent it all back to me. This only created more unsettled feelings in me and I am certain my student teacher must have picked up the tension subconsciously as well.

Another factor which I feel added to some of the new students' slow growth was the fact that they had such a pile-up of negative feelings and emotions to let go of. Through the daily meditations they gradually learned to change their emotions and feelings at will. It wasn't until later in the year, however, that they were able to get real inner control over these emotions, enough control to really manifest a steady change in their outward behavior.

In December I began to notice some real changes in the way some of the children were relating to one another. During the first week of December, Danielle, the child who had been passed from aunt to aunt, had her first few positive days all year. After this she began to express the positive side of her personality more of the time. About this same time, Rosa, one of Danielle's friends, also began to become more positive. I often felt for Rosa, who was a large boisterous girl for her age, because she spent long hours at home in the evenings without parent supervision, and she was only in the *third* grade! She was not the only child in the class who spent evenings alone, unsupervised. Towards the end of December, Rosa, Danielle, and Noni, who were friends but who fought almost daily, began to fight less. Chapter fifteen, which deals with Creative Conflict and problem solving, gives a more detailed account of these girls' conflicts and how both meditation and Creative Conflict helped them work through their conflicts.

In January some of the children such as Brian, began to be able to keep their bodies still and quiet for the first time all year during meditation. This resulted in their having more control over themselves both inside the classroom and on the playground. Simultaneously, they became more concentrated in academic tasks and began to feel better about themselves. As this happened they became more sensitive and caring about other people's feelings.

Some of the parents of children in the class expressed how they saw their children change because of the centering meditations. Sharon's mother said, "Sharon has changed tremendously since entering your class. I know for sure that centering is partly responsible. She has grown in self-assurance and self-confidence. She enjoys herself and is not as withdrawn. I really enjoy the new Sharon and she likes herself." Rex, a pushy, aggressive student who entered the class towards the end of the school year, became cooperative after participating in centering for about a month. His mother said that Rex talked about centering at home. "He thinks it's very good for getting control of your emotions and helping everybody to concentrate better. He has calmed down quite a bit. He doesn't get into heated arguments anymore. I think it has been very good for him."

Roger, who had been in the class for two years, grew a lot in his ability to control his emotions. He had a reputation for throwing rocks in fits of anger and pulling hair out of other children's heads. His mother expressed, "Roger has always had a hard time controlling his temper. Sometimes he will use centering to help himself. Just having it as a tool to use is a help to him."

Bill's mother said, "Bill tries to use centering when he is angry or depressed. He seems to have a more positive approach to his work. I think he is developing a better self-image through his use of centering."

On March 13, 1979, for the first time I began to notice the class begin to come together as a cohesive group. Here is what I wrote in my journal: "This week I am noticing that the class is beginning to gel. I feel the warm peaceful feelings during the meditations that I often felt last year. There seems to be more calm and quiet in the meditation time and during the school day. It seems the class is finally gaining some sense of unity and group consciousness."

The change in the children was beautiful to experience. During the last three months of school (in which children usually tend to become more restless and difficult to handle) the class increased in self-discipline, respect, and concern for others. It became such a rewarding class to work with that I felt a deep sadness as the school year came to an end. Back at the shaky start of the year I certainly did not expect to feel this way at the end.

I believe that every classroom can experience this same wondrous growth through meditation to a new sense of caring and peace. The wonderful thing about using meditation is that it takes no time-consuming preparation but produces dramatic results with regular practice. In closing this chapter I would like to share how one little girl one morning expressed her caring for another just before flag salute when we put our hands over our hearts. She tenderly exclaimed, "My heart is beating fast for Sonya's birthday."

Children send energy to the plants in their garden.

CHAPTER 9

Energy

Deborah Rozman, in *Meditating With Children*, suggests that in teaching meditation to children, the teacher start by discussing energy, what it is, where it comes from and where it goes to. She encourages the teacher to have the children practice sending and then withdrawing energy from each of the body parts in turn. During breathing exercises she suggests that the teacher have the students draw in fresh life force and energy with the breath from a source outside themselves.

I have found that children who meditate regularly are very sensitive to energy flows in themselves, in others, in plants and animals, and in the environment around them. In class we often channel energy to plants through our hands. Many students are able to tune into the energy in plants and to tell what the plant needs.* Last September, I brought four wilting house plants to class. We tuned in to see what the plants needed. The children came up with different needs for each plant ranging from water to the need for a larger pot. In the next few days we gave each plant what the children had divined. The children's perceptions seemed to be accurate, as the plants regained health quickly.

---

*Peter Tomkins, *The Secret Life of Plants* (New York: Harper and Row, 1973.)

One May afternoon, Tom, the gardener, told Anthony that if he talked to his (Anthony's) newly planted seedlings, they would hear and grow better. That afternoon the children and I sent energy to our seedlings. Then we sent energy through our hands to a person in the center of the circle, giving those who wanted to, a chance to be in the center. A hush fell over the children as we sent energy to one another. Afterwards, Phil said he felt the energy coming into himself and he built a force field around himself with it so that if any bad energy came near him it would dissolve. Ellen said, "I saw a red dot and line going to the plant and to the people I was sending energy to." She expressed that she could actually feel the energy the class sent to her face which was badly scraped in a bicycle accident.

As in Ellen's case, children often experience flows of energy in the form of images. These images are often very rich in color and movement, and can be quite complex. Every morning I have the children imagine they are filling up with fresh new energy from the universe. Sometimes I have them imagine that energy is pouring down through their heads and filling their whole bodies. The children often report feeling the energy inside themselves and enjoy sharing their experiences.

One morning following meditation, Don said, "It felt like I had a balloon of energy all around me." On another morning Tim said, "When I filled up with energy I felt like a bottle filling up with water." Such images seem to be common to all young children no matter what age. Don and Tim were students in my second-grade class. The following year my third graders experienced similar images from the same meditation. Brian, one of these third-graders described his experience, "I could really feel the energy going out and coming in." Another third-grader, Alan said, "I feel like I have a bottle on each side, one filled with love and one filled with energy. All the fresh love and energy comes in to the bottles and all the old energy goes out." Phil, also in third grade, shared that the energy felt like waves crashing in front of him.

Sometimes we felt this type of energy strongly as a whole group. In one meditation as a group we all experienced an especially powerful feeling of peace and energy entering our bodies. It all started when I bought one of those huge paper rainbows for the birthday of a

"This plant needs a drink."

treasured person in my life. I had bought it early and was saving it for my friend when I came to discover he already had one. The question arose, "What to do with the rainbow?" After tossing the decision about in my head a bit, I decided to give it to the children. I brought it to school one morning and Tanya, my aide, and I carefully mounted it on cardboard and placed it on a large table. Ten minutes later, the children entered. Soon the room was filled with excited voices and many questions. "Where did you get the rainbow? Where are you going to put it?" After morning meditation I asked the children where they would like to put their new rainbow. Joseph expressed that he would like to hang it above our meditation rug. He declared, "We can send it energy and then whenever someone feels bad they can go sit under the rainbow and it will make them feel good." Everyone agreed that this was what they wanted to do with the rainbow. During recess my aide and I hung the huge rainbow from the lights above the meditation rug. After lunch I led the children through a meditation in which I had them imagine they were rainbows. At the end of the meditation I had them all send energy to the rainbow above the rug. Many children raised their hands up to the rainbow as they sent it energy. A parent walked in, quietly, smiling and she whispered a message to her son. The children were so absorbed they did not hear her or lose concentration.

Some of the children began to use centering at home to help themselves become re-charged with energy when they were tired. One afternoon, Tammie said, "I do centering at home every Tuesday when I come home from dance class. I get tired and my legs get weak. Then after centering I have more energy to do things." Joseph also found he could re-charge himself through centering. He expressed one morning, "When I get tired I go in my room and relax and then I have more energy. I imagine energy is coming in. It helps me through the day 'cause it gives me energy."

The children not only became more aware of their energy but became aware of the deep effects relaxation had on their bodies. They often mentioned how relaxed they felt following a meditation, often expressing these feelings in images. And what images! They are a delight!

"We can send the rainbow energy."

Anna—I felt like I was butter melting.
Tim—I felt like a big huge heavy rock sinking.
Rochelle—I felt so relaxed I felt like I was floating.
Tina—My eyes were so relaxed I couldn't feel them.
Steve—I felt like water falling into the rug.
Rick—My fingers felt like they weren't even there.
Don—I had a scratch on my head and I couldn't scratch it because I was so relaxed.
Jeannie—I felt all tingly, like bubbly relaxation was flowing all the way down my body.

In becoming more aware of energy and of their own states of relaxation the children begin to use meditation to help themselves when they are hurt or sick. In the same way that the children learn to send energy to seedlings and plants, they begin to learn to use energy and the meditation process to help their own bodies. Here is what I wrote in my journal about one little eight-year-old girl: "Yesterday Melissa went home with a fever; to my surprise she came back to school today. She said, 'I centered on my bed and imagined I was better. I did it all day. I'm glad because I could come back to school today.'"

Don, also an eight-year-old, told how he helped himself feel better after a bad fall from his bike: "Once when I was riding my bike I jumped over this ramp and I went real high and I landed real far away. My front tire ran into a mailbox and I just went flat down on the street. I cut my arm and so I went home and did centering and I felt a whole lot better."

During morning centering, usually at least one child would speak up in this way to tell how he or she had used centering to help a cut, bruise, burn or sprained ankle. Tim shared a heart-warming account of how he turned his energies around after an injury. "I was on my way to a swimming party with my friend. I was hurrying, running, because he and his mom were down in my front yard in the car. They were going to drive us, my sister and I. So I was running down the stairs real super, super fast. I accidentally tripped over a book because my brother cleaned up his closet and threw out all the books and one landed on the stairs. After I tripped over the book I accidentally sprained my ankle and my right arm got cut. It was bleeding and I couldn't go swimming and I had to stay and watch them go. I couldn't go. That made me feel kind of sad. I did centering at home and it made me feel a lot better."

The reason the children were able to make themselves feel better is because imagination has the power to shape reality. So when they hurt themselves, they were not just pretending they were better; they actually felt better. In the same way that meditation changes the energy flows in the classroom, centering at times of physical injury is able to affect the energy flows in the body, and the children can feel these changes.

Tina, an active, talkative eight-year-old with a temper, found she could be more in control of her energies through centering when dealing with her younger sister who teased her a lot. She said, "Ellie was bugging me. She wanted me to play school and was going to hit me in the stomach if I didn't play. So I went into the den when no one was there and did imagination experience. Then I felt better. When I do it she can't bug me anymore, what she says doesn't bother me anymore and I say, 'You can't bother me.'"

Roberta, a very timid seven-year-old, told how she was scared because her mother's boyfriend was going to spank her. She said, "I went into my secret hide-out and centered. I felt much better afterwards."

In all of these incidences the children were aware of and more in control of their own energies after centering. Children who meditate regularly learn that they can change their energy at will. What a gift this will be when carried into their adult lives.

What does it mean to be able to change your energy at will? What *is* the will? The will is the part of us that says yes to life—yes I will take on this challenge, yes I will resolve this conflict; I will accept life's pains and keep on trying. For children, it means finding a great reservoir of strength inside a small immature body. It means forgiving those who call you "flat face". It means coming to school with a smile even though you have difficulty learning. And most of all, it means facing the greatest challenge of all—the courage to be yourself.

Children get excited about the live "visitors".

CHAPTER 10

Teaching Science Through the Imagination

So often the curriculum of schools does not reach the deeper being of the students but only fills the mind for a little while. When we teach through imagination, we take the child to a deeper level of his consciousness than either the memory or the intellect or the conceptual faculty can take him. The imagination makes an impression that is seen and felt and directly experienced. Just as the vivid moments of our lives are unforgettable, so too is learning through the imagination. Once you realize the power of this imaginative faculty, science can be one of the most exciting subjects you teach.

My classroom is usually blessed with a few snakes, lizards, or other creatures of nature. Science lessons come alive when you have the real thing to observe and discover. Children have a natural love and curiosity for their environment and for all the living creatures in it. They are capable of becoming very caring and sensitive to insects, plants and animals. I find meditation a wonderful tool to enhance this sensitivity.

Although I have a regular science program, we often deviate from the daily plan to explore some new live visitor in our room. One warmish January day Scott brought a frog to class. During the last hour of the morning we all gathered on the rug to take a good look at the young frog. The children excitedly told all they knew about frogs.

I then grabbed from the shelf my Childcraft Volume on Animals and read to the children, giving them a clearer picture of how a frog emerges from a tadpole. After lunch I led the children through the first steps of meditation: yoga exercises, relaxing the body, and breathing to inhale good feelings and let go of negative ones. I then led the children through a guided fantasy, having them imagine they were tadpoles swimming in a pond. I had them imagine what it would feel like to breathe with gills, live in a pond, and play with other tadpoles. Then I had them grow arms and legs, develop lungs and eventually turn into frogs. The children really enjoyed the experience. Afterwards several children gave the name of the frog they had become. The emotional and motivational climate for learning was very pregnant and the children gathered quickly around me to look at pictures of frogs and hear more about them.

I find that giving the children a chance to experience something in their imagination enhances the learning process. The children actually identify with and become the thing we are studying, and this makes the topic come alive for them. Learning becomes internal instead of external, personal instead of impersonal. It seems far better to have a child imagine he is the wind than to have him only read about it from a textbook. The textbook can be used later, to get facts and information which you or the child may be curious about, but you first must capture the child's motivation and interest. Having the children imagine they are frogs, snakes, lizards, or whatever, brings out all the wonderful curiosity and excitement you will ever need to help learning occur. For this reason I often begin science lessons with a meditation. The water meditation from *Meditating With Children* is an excellent meditation to do before a science lesson on water. Actually, you can begin any academic or creative lesson with a meditation. The rewards are to have students more deeply in touch with the subject of study and more fully motivated. The water meditation mentioned above works very well before a watercolor or finger painting class. Meditation can be used before social studies, history, creative movement, dance and drama. There are endless possibilities. All it requires is a little creativity on the teacher's part.

One of my favorite guided fantasies which I use in teaching science is to have the children imagine they are a seed in the moist earth, experiencing all the stages of growth until they are a beautiful flower.

After experiencing this in our imaginations, then we act it out with the physical body. What fun! The children simply love these experiences.

In one guided fantasy in which the children grew from seed to flower I asked the children to imagine how the rain, wind and sun would feel on them. How would they communicate with other plants? When it was over, Anthony's eyes sparkled, "Wow, that was neat!" Several children said they became trees and grew fruit that someone came to pick. Steve said his branches were used to build a boat. Jeannie smiled, "I was a plant and many flowers grew on me." Rick expressed that he communicated with other plants by antennae on his leaves. Phil said he wouldn't like not being able to walk. Anthony told how he was able to pinch people if they tried to pick his flowers. Melissa and Joseph said they liked it when people smelled their flowers. Tim's flower came out to be a rose which surprised him. The excitement in the children was wonderful to feel. We went on to explore the parts of a flower, the pistil, stamen, petals and roots.

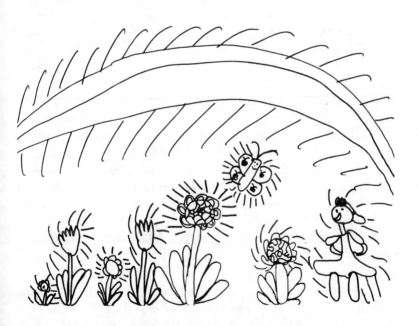

The child senses energy in all of nature.

As you can see, not all of what the children experience in the imagination is exactly accurate scientifically. The imagination tends to run in its own creative direction at times. The child does, however, internalize the essence feeling of what he is learning about, and he is highly motivated to learn more.

Here is a guided fantasy which I have found very successful for teaching evaporation and condensation. As you read through it, picture in your mind what it would be like to be a child, deeply relaxed with eyes closed, learning in this way: "You are a beautiful lake. You are cool, fresh and clean. You are so clear that you are like a mirror, and the clouds, sky, and trees are reflected in you. Now imagine you are just one small drop of water in the lake, sitting on the smooth surface of the water. The sun shines down on you, warming you, and you leave the pond, becoming one with the air. No one can see you because you are so small. You travel through the air—up and up until you are quite high. Now you are very high, looking down on the earth below you. You notice other tiny invisible drops of water just like you all around you. You all gather closer and closer together. You are now a drop of water in a cloud. All the other droplets are part of the cloud, too. Now imagine that you are the whole cloud. Feel what it is like to have the sun shining on you from above. Feel the wind blow you in different directions. How does this make you feel? Imagine that an airplane is flying through you. Look down now upon the earth and see all you can see. Now become a tiny droplet of water again. Begin to fall down, down, down. This does not scare you; you fall down gently. Other droplets are falling all around you. You dance and play in the wind as you fall down. Now you are very close to the earth. Where do you fall and what happens to you next?" I led my class in this exercise one rainy December afternoon. Nearly everyone wanted to share what they imagined. Half the class wanted to do it all over again. Several closed their eyes, ready to begin again. I told them I was very pleased that they enjoyed it so much and that we did not have time today but would do it again the next day, which we did!

The class was now ripe for discussion. I asked questions to see what the children had learned from their experience. We discussed the meanings of the words "condensation" and "evaporation" and I answered any questions about facts the children were not clear on. We then looked at some charts and I read several pages to the children from a book about weather. The children's excitement and interest remained high throughout the lesson. The children then asked if they could do some experiments from their science book, illustrating these principles, which we did the following afternoon. The whole lesson culminated with a movie on Friday about clouds.

Here are a few stories written by the third-graders at the beginning of one year in connection with the evaporation condensation meditation. Actually they were written during creative writing time, not science time. Although each child's creativity expressed itself a bit differently you can see the basic understanding of the process of condensation and evaporation which these children had gained.

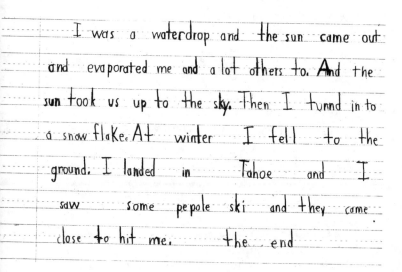

I was a waterdrop and the sun came out and evaporated me and a lot others to. And the sun took us up to the sky. Then I turnd in to a snow flake. At winter I fell to the ground. I landed in Tahoe and I saw some pepole ski and they came close to hit me. the end

When I was a rain-drop I eveporated up into the air. I became part of a cloud. It was so cold up in the sky I froze. Then I became a snowflake. I flew down from the sky like a angel. When I fell down I became prettyer and prettyer.

I was a snowflake. I was the littlest snowflake ever. I liked being little because everybody came to see me. My name is Flaker, I am blue. I went around the world two times. Finally the sun melted me away. Now I'm a pile of snow.

The following stories from the same meditation were recorded in my journal so they do not appear in the children's original handwriting.

"*If I were a raindrop I would fill up dry rivers and
make people say, 'Here comes rain today. It will be a
rainy day today.' *"

"*One day I disintegrated up to a cloud. There were
a bunch of raindrops up in the cloud with me. I was
squashed. I looked down. I screamed, 'Help.' In fact
I fell on a horse's back. One day the horse ran. I fell
off him onto a beautiful flower. I helped the flower
grow very high.*"

At several intervals during the year I check the children's retention
of these lessons. Five months after this set of lessons, most children
could still describe in detail the process of condensation and evaporation. I believe retention is enhanced by the fact that the children had
experienced the process in their imagination. It had not only become
something interesting to learn about but had become a personal
experience, something the children could identify with.

One week in March we had three different kinds of animals visit
our class consecutively for three days, making for some exciting
learning. Whenever a new animal is brought to class, we first sit on the
rug giving everyone a chance to get a good look at it. We then close
our eyes, relax, breathe, focus our minds, and become the animal now
sitting in the middle of the rug. On Monday we all became lizards, on
Tuesday snakes and on Wednesday rabbits. After the guided imagery
was over on Wednesday I asked the children how imagining they were
a rabbit was different from imagining they were a snake or lizard. Rick
said it was difficult being a snake because he could feel the ground as
he slid on it, while in being a rabbit he only hopped. Don expressed
that he preferred being a rabbit because he liked having fur. Ellen
smiled, "I would rather be a snake because then I could hibernate in
the winter." Tom said lizards were different from both the snake and
the rabbit because chameleons could change colors. Because the
children had internalized the experiences of being a snake, a lizard,
and a rabbit, it became fun for them to compare and see the likeness
and differences between these three animals. They were exploring life
from inside out.

The children were so highly motivated by this spontaneous study
of animals that I suggested they read about their favorite animal and
write a report. With great interest and perseverance my class of

second-graders set out to do their reports. It took them several days to complete the reports. This was the first time I experienced second-graders writing such comprehensive reports. Here are two of them.

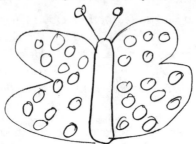

Butterflies are the most beautiful insect. They like to fly in the sky. A butterfly has three parts. All butterflies are

different than the others. All butterflies aren't the same colors. All Butterflies are different colors. They live all over the world and some

butterflies live very long lives.

Snakes

Snakes are cold blooded. their blood is about the same temperature as the air around them or soil.

Some snakes sleep through the winter. Some snakes are hatched from eggs. Some snakes eat rats and bugs.

Some snakes are very big. Snakes find The cement or blacktop warmer than The ground.
The end

"Did you know that whales do not have ears on the outside but they can still hear?"

Many science lessons develop from the requests of the children. Roger asked if we could imagine being dolphins one morning. At lunch time that day I read all I could about dolphins. I incorporated many facts about dolphins that afternoon as I led the class in meditation. The children loved it and were anxious to share their experiences. They were full of questions about dolphins afterwards, so we huddled together and read about them.

I sometimes discover through our science meditations that children are carrying around scientific misconceptions which lead to fascinating discussions. In February we studied a unit about stars and planets. Several days before I planned to show a movie about stars, I had the children imagine they were a star, during afternoon meditation. I had them imagine what color star they would be and what size and shape they would have. The children really enjoyed the meditation. Afterwards we shared. Rick's star was as small as a ball and when humans touched it, it burned them. Jim had a blue star; Don's was yellow. Many children had spikes on their stars. Realizing the children had no awareness of what stars really looked like, I drew some pictures on the chalkboard. Rick asked, "Then why do people draw them with spikes?" His question led us into an exciting lesson on symbols and how they are used to represent natural things.

The range of topics that can be meditated on as part of a science lesson is endless. My students have enjoyed becoming the ocean, the earth, the sun, a snowflake, a waterfall, a rock, the whole universe, and many other images from nature. A good image to work with is that of a salmon being born in a river, traveling downstream to the sea, and returning upstream to lay its eggs. If you have a lightning and thunderstorm you can become the storm. There are numerous possibilities just waiting to be explored.

Wonder!

CHAPTER 11

Imagination: Creator of Reality

Some people look down on the faculty of imagination and feel that it deals with unrealities. As you can see from the previous chapter, the imagination can be a great help in one of the most difficult real-world tasks— the teaching of difficult scientific material to small children. But to regard the imagination primarily as a tool, a handy technique to use or not to use, is to miss its real significance.

The imagination is a very powerful part of us, a most important part of our being, often neglected in our public schools because educators fail to recognize its value. The imagination affects all other levels of learning because they are all dependent on how the learner imagines himself. If a child views himself as slow and unintelligent he will manifest this image and not be capable of much learning. In the same way, if a child sees himself as sharp and capable he will have confidence and learn easily. The second child may not be in truth more capable than the first child, he only has the image of being a successful learner and therefore lives up to this image and tries hard to learn.

The sad part is that children are often told by an older sibling, a parent, or a teacher that they are not capable of doing certain things. The trusting child believes the elder authority and may never attempt to develop a certain part of himself, simply because he believed an untrue statement from another and incorporated this statement into his image of himself. This happened to me as a child. My older sister who played the piano well would seldom let me sing along with the rest of my brothers and sisters because she said I was always off key. This gave me a lot of pain because I loved to sing. I believed something was wrong with me and after that I seldom attempted to sing, especially if others were present close by. About four years ago I joined the chanting choir at the University of the Trees*. In an audition to join the choir I was told I was tone deaf and should stay on one note during the chanting sessions. For a long time I did not practice because I believed I was incapable of learning the scales. Eventually I was confronted with a choice: I must either practice or leave the choir. So I began to practice daily, still not convinced that I could learn what I was practicing. After about six months of daily practice, however, I began to hear the scales in my mind and I could then reproduce with my voice what I was hearing in my mind. You can imagine my excitement. Chanting with the choir has become a deeply fulfilling experience for me, but it took a long time to reprogram the image I had created of myself when my sister told me I could not sing. Many children grow up with such false images of themselves seriously limiting their true potential.

This is why I believe meditation and development of the imagination are so important to children. We have the responsibility to help children create positive images of themselves because the images they have of themselves, conscious or unconscious, create and mold their reality. If they view themselves as failures, then they will likely grow up and manifest as failures. If they see themselves as leaders, as people who can skillfully manifest and take responsibility, then they will more likely grow up and do something worthwhile with their lives.

A main quality of the imagination is a sense of wonder, a sense of awe for the whole universe we are part of. This sense of wonder is so alive in children! Remember when you were young how one day sometimes felt as long as a whole week, or how the sun dancing on the dew in the morning seemed so magical? The whole world was wonderful and you couldn't wait to see what was going to happen next. You felt like you could climb any mountain or do anything you set your mind to do. Your imagination was very much alive in you in

---

*University of the Trees, a university founded and directed by Dr. Christopher Hills, which conducts research into human awareness and human potential located in Boulder Creek, CA.

Heroes together—alive and free.

this young age and the sense of being a hero was alive in your imagination. It is this part of adults which leads them to do heroic deeds and bring real change into the world. And it is this part which often dies in children in our public schools long before they reach adulthood. The child's image of himself changes as he progresses through the grades. He no longer feels that sense of awe for the universe, or that he can conquer any challenge set before him. The light goes out in his eyes.

I have experienced the hero begin to die in a child as early as first grade. My first year of teaching, twelve years ago, was in a public school in northern California. I recall the children entering the class full of excitement, wonder, and a deep yearning to learn. The school had certain books to teach from and certain ways that the children were to be taught. But these methods did not allow space for the individual child and the need of children to learn at their own pace. As the children tried to mold themselves to a specific way of learning, they began to change. They became less enthusiastic, and the joy and yearning to learn, with which they entered the class, began to die away. There was no space in the curriculum for their imaginations and feelings, their true creative potential. They were molding themselves to a system which ignored much of their beings. It pained me to watch their enthusiasm die. After watching the spark die in the first-graders, I knew why children are so often turned off to school by the time they get to the upper grades. It all begins during their first years of school.

The wonderful thing about the imagination is that through it a person has the power to transform his whole reality. Whatever we image in our imagination is what our reality will be. We can change any negative image we have of ourselves to a positive healthy image and turn our whole life around in a positive way. Alan, the boy mentioned in chapter three turned an image of low self-confidence and failure into one of quiet self-confidence and success. His actual image of himself changed. You could see this in the expression on his face and in the way he carried his body. Once he changed his image of himself, he began to walk and express himself in a totally new way. He no longer looked worried or anxious but now often radiated a joyful smile. He lost the clumsy way he moved his body and began to walk with self-confidence. The way he imagined himself deeply affected how he used his body, either for positive or negative. As Alan's image of himself changed, he became more and more successful in his manifestation in class, and his relationship with his peers improved.

Through meditation children can be taught to willfully create images of beauty, goodness and success. We can help them learn to master their imagination and have true creative power over their lives. It all starts with small steps, basically showing them that they can purposefully use the power of their imaginations to change bad feelings to good feelings, to picture themselves doing well in something and then succeeding. There are many examples in the chapters to follow, of how children learned to use their imaginations through meditation to transform their images of themselves and their feelings about painful situations in their lives. In each case the children were learning to use their image-making faculty for a constructive purpose. They were gaining an invaluable skill, a skill which they often began to apply to the whole of their lives.

Within the imagination lies the image-making process. Actually, we see everything in images. When you look at a tree, signals are passing from your eyes along your nervous system into your brain. The image of the tree is then re-created from these signals in the imagination. You don't really *see* the tree—you re-create the image of the tree in your imagination. This image-making process is vital to

education. Imagine trying to read without being able to visualize or create pictures of what you are reading in your imagination. Even the words on the page are images, images of symbols which are interpreted in the imagination. Many children come to school with their visualizing process stifled. They are so bombarded by modern media and television, which present the viewer with images already created, so that the viewer does not adequately develop his own natural image-making ability. Even if the imagination is very much alive, as it is naturally in the very young child, it soon becomes limited through non-use. Every year I seemed to have more and more children enter my class who had serious reading difficulties. I believe part of the cause was the lack of development of the child's imagination due to over-exposure to modern media. I believe meditation helps alleviate this problem because it helps re-open this natural image-making capacity.

Bob, a spunky lovable mischievous seven-year-old, comes to mind. He had his own television in his bedroom and was allowed to watch many hours of television from a very young age. He entered my second-grade class with very poor reading skills. It took almost a whole year for Bob to regain his visualizing ability through meditation. Once he began to be able to visualize he learned to read very quickly, making up for several years of lost time. By the end of the third grade he was reading at grade level, as recorded on the Stanford Achievement Tests.*

Many other academic subjects learned in our schools are also dependent on or enhanced by the imagination. The ability to use one's imagination is crucial in solving certain types of math problems, particularly word problems. Geometry, trigonometry and calculus—all call upon the imagination of the learner. Our great scientists use the genius of their imaginations as they uncover more and more of the secrets of the universe. Recently, in some schools, the learning of spelling words and math facts has been enhanced by using the image-making process. Harris Clemens, Ph.D., is pioneering such work with children in Santa Cruz County. He discovered that fifth-graders who practiced their spelling words by closing their eyes and imaging a magic chalkboard in their minds, on which they wrote their spelling words in their favorite color of magic chalk, could easily beat sixth-graders in the same school who learned through traditional methods in spelling bees. I applied this technique of the imagination in my own classroom, teaching the children to lead one another in the magic chalkboard visualization process. My children loved to learn in this way, many of them learning many spelling words per week. Parents also enjoyed this new method of teaching spelling and often helped their children at home with it. I usually led the children in a short

---

*Stanford Achievement Tests are standardized tests used to record children's progress in academic skills. They are usually given at the beginning and at the end of each school year.

meditation before they did this type of spelling practice, so they could begin the practice from a calm, focused state of mind.

The creative arts are also quite dependent on the imagination. The composer hears the musical piece in his imagination before he records it on musical scores or plays it on an instrument. The artist conceives his painting in his imagination before he paints it on canvas. The imagination plays a vital role in creative dramatics and dance. The poet and writer also bring to us an inner experience born from the imagination. I found meditation a definite key in helping children open and express this type of creativity.

And what about the school of business? I used to think business was boring and uncreative and that I would never want to study business. That was before I became involved in the common owner-ship business at the University of the Trees Press. I have come to realize through my involvement in the business that some of the people who are the greatest assets to the business are those who use their imaginations skillfully and who are able to bring the images in their imaginations down to concrete reality, enhancing the business with fresh creative ideas.

The imagination is a truly marvelous part of our beings. We hardly realize its importance in creating our lives.* Meditation became a vital tool in my classroom for building and, in some cases, opening the children's beautifully natural imaginations. It was like opening the bud of a flower and experiencing its true beauty, a beauty rare and precious and wonderful to behold. Children's imaginations never fail to be a source of pure delight.

---

*To read further about the incredible power of the imagination to create and re-create our environment and even the cells of our own body, read *Nuclear Evolution*, by Christopher Hills,(Boulder Creek, CA: University of the Trees Press, 1977.)

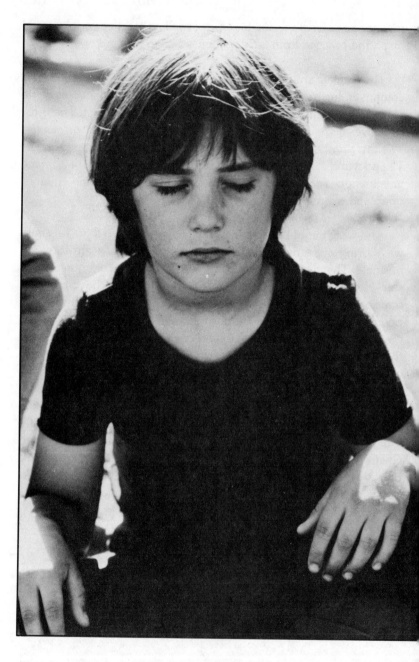

"A wave of relaxation flows down over my face."

Beautiful Meditations

Many of the highly imaginative meditations which follow were made up spontaneously, depending upon what season of the year it was or what was happening in the classroom at the time. The more you capture the children's imagination in meditation, the more they will enjoy and be able to fully participate. A meditation such as the jack-o-lantern meditation works very well with children from kindergarten through about fifth grade because it starts out with an image children all love. After becoming a jack-o-lantern, they easily are able to expand the image of the candle light extending to the whole of space.

These meditations should not be done without the basic beginning steps outlined in Deborah Rozman's book *Meditating With Children* and mentioned in chapter four. These include tensing and relaxing of the physical body, getting in touch with feelings, followed by rhythmic breathing to release old feelings and recharge with new fresh life force, energy and feelings. Following the meditations are some of the children's pictures, stories, responses, or my comments on their responses which I recorded in my journal.

WATERFALL RELAXATION

(I used this relaxation routine at times to help the children relax before meditation. This is a variation on the "tensing and relaxing of the body" step.)

A beautiful waterfall of white light is falling down on you. It splashes down on your head, helping your head to relax. You feel your head relaxing. It moves down over your neck and shoulders. Your neck and shoulders are relaxing. It flows down your back. Your back is letting go and relaxing. It flows over your chest and stomach, helping your chest and stomach relax. You feel your chest and stomach relax. Now it falls down over your arms. You feel your arms relaxing. It splashes down over your buttocks and abdomen. You feel them relax. It moves down over your legs and feet. You feel your legs and feet letting go and relaxing. The beautiful waterfall of white light is flowing over your whole body. You are very peaceful and relaxed. Here are a few of the children's images of the waterfall relaxation:

Rochelle—"When you said the waterfall, I imagined and saw flowers coming down on me, in all pretty colors, on top of the waterfall. Later on, I had all these bubbles going down on me."

Tina—"The waterfall part made me feel real relaxed. I didn't even want to open my eyes."

Tim—"I was in a gold mine, walking along in it, and all this gold came gushing down on me, and that was my waterfall, and it felt really good."

RAINBOW MEDITATION

Feel your body becoming lighter and lighter. See all the colors of the rainbow. Feel your body becoming all of the colors of the rainbow. Feel your body becoming all the colors of light in the rainbow: red, orange, yellow, green, blue, indigo and violet. You are the rainbow, your colors streaming out in every direction. Feel yourself getting bigger and bigger, your colors streaming out farther and farther. Your colors of light are spreading farther and farther until they cover this whole room, then even farther until they cover the whole city, and still farther until they cover the whole earth. You spread out even farther and become even bigger. Now your colors of light are spreading throughout the whole universe. You are as big as the whole universe, your colors of light shining out in every direction in space and touching all of space.

The following are the children's responses to the rainbow meditation, as described in my journal:

Alan drew a picture after this meditation of himself in his favorite clothes. He colored the clothes in his picture all the colors of the rainbow. He drew a rainbow over the picture of himself. Some children expressed that they slid down the rainbow in their meditations. One seven-year-old girl expressed that half her rainbow was a person with a rainbow body so she could slide down the rainbow. Another girl said "hello" to an airplane which flew by. A star scratched the back of Roger's rainbow. Roberta jumped off her rainbow into a helicopter. Rick said the rainbow made him wet. Mary fell off her rainbow. Melissa flew up in the clouds, became the sun and then fell down and became a rainbow. Laura saw a rainbow with all the colors in it except black. Anthony's rainbow was a roller coaster he could ride on. A few days after the rainbow meditation eight-year-old Joseph wrote this: "What makes a rainbow? After a shower you can see a rainbow in the sky if the sun is shining but the air is still filled with raindrops, though sunlight looks white."

Many times I have been impressed at the profound level of contemplative thought the children reach following a meditation. They probe the secrets of nature and the essence of rocks, birds, animals, water, rainbows—whatever image from nature that we use in the meditation. I firmly believe that meditation on a subject brings out a true love of learning and scientific inquiry from even the youngest children. The teacher's challenge is then to direct this open and questing mind into avenues for learning and creativity. Meditation establishes the attitude that fosters rapid learning and creative learning.

On the following pages are a few pictures and stories produced by third-grade children following the rainbow meditation which exemplify this creativity.

Once I saw a
rainbow. It was a
beautiful rainbow and
in the morning
I found my self as
a rainbow amd I
was all sorts of
colors. I saw my
friend and she saw me
in the morning. I
made her as a rainbow.
She went up with me.
up up up and up.

I was a rainbow and my colors
were green yellow and orange red
blue and I was a pretty
rainbow and everybody like my
pretty colors I had one
litte girl who was crying so
I went over and I told
her to hope on my back
and so she did.

BUTTERFLY MEDITATION

Pretend that you are a beautiful butterfly. What kind of butterfly are you? See the colors and patterns on your wings. You move your wings gently and feel yourself take off and fly. You fly to a nearby flower. You use your antennae to smell the flower. Now suck up the sweet nectar of the flower with your antennae. Fully refreshed, you are ready to fly. You fly higher and higher up to the tree tops. You dance between the leaves of the trees. Now you see another butterfly which looks just like you. You dance together in the warm sunlight. You communicate with one another with your antennae. Filled with the joy and beauty of the world around, you land gently on the flower to rest. You are thankful for the opportunity for life.

Variation on the Butterfly Meditation

You can have the children pretend that they, as a butterfly, become magic and can fly up higher and higher into space until they fly to the outermost limits of space. This type of meditation gives the children a feeling of expansion. The children drew some beautiful pictures of butterflies following this meditation.

METAMORPHOSIS MEDITATION

You are a tiny egg laying under a milkweed leaf. You are the size of a dew drop. You feel yourself hatching into a tiny caterpillar. You begin to crawl around on the milkweed leaf. You are hungry, so you begin to eat the leaf. You eat and eat and grow bigger and bigger. Soon you discover your skin is too tight. Your old skin bursts and you crawl out of it, wearing a brand new skin. You feel happy in your soft new skin. You crawl around eating more and more leaves growing larger and larger. Soon you don't fit in your skin again. It bursts and again you crawl out with a brand new soft skin. You eat more and more leaves, shedding your skin two more times, each time crawling out with a brand new skin. One day you decide it is time to rest and you spin a button of silk on a twig. You hang downward from the twig, held by the button of silk for a whole day. You feel yourself changing. You have a special shell now to protect you. It is called a chrysalis. It is bright and gold-trimmed. You stay in it for two weeks. All this time you quietly grow and change. One day the chrysalis splits and you come out but you now look like a butterfly. At first you are wet and weak but the warm sun quickly helps you dry off your wings. You take off for your first flight. Up into the sky you fly higher and higher. You are now a beautiful tawny brown butterfly.

Notice the chrysalis hanging from the tree.

COLOR MEDITATION

Breathe in the color red. You are becoming the color red. Your whole body is red. What does it feel like to be the color red?

Breathe in the color orange. You are becoming the color orange. Your whole body is orange. What does it feel like to be the color orange?

Breathe in the color yellow. You are becoming the color yellow. Your whole body is yellow. What does it feel like to be the color yellow?

Breathe in the color green. Your whole body is green. What does it feel like to be the color green?

Breathe in the color blue. You are becoming the color blue. Your whole body is blue. What does it feel like to be the color blue?

Breathe in the color indigo. You are becoming the color indigo. Your whole body is indigo. What does it feel like to be the color indigo?

Breathe in the color violet. You are becoming the color violet. Your whole body is violet. What does it feel like to be the color violet?

Children's responses:

> After this meditation the children wanted to share their experiences. One boy imagined he was a lizard which could change colors. Some children saw different images as they breathed in the colors. Rick saw oranges for the color orange, apples for red and green, and he saw bananas for yellow. One child saw the colors as colored ants marching along.

JACK-O-LANTERN MEDITATION
(For Halloween)

Imagine that you are a pumpkin growing in a field. A child comes and takes you home. The child carves you into a wonderful jack-o-lantern and puts a candle inside you. On Halloween night the child lights the candle. A beautiful light begins to shine inside you; it gets brighter and brighter. It begins to shine out of your eyes, nose, and mouth. You shine so brightly, you begin to shine over the whole city, out onto all the people and houses. You get brighter and brighter. You begin to shine out over the whole world. You become ever brighter and begin to shine out over the whole universe, shining past the planets out to the stars. You shine on the stars and between the stars. You shine out to the whole of space.

Children's responses:

The children in my classes loved to do this meditation during the Halloween season. They would ask to do it every day.

WIND MEDITATION
(Good for windy days)

Listen to the wind. What does it sound like? How does it make you feel? Feel the wind on your face. Imagine you are becoming the wind. Feel yourself blowing and blowing. Feel yourself blowing on trees and buildings. Feel yourself blowing through trees. Feel yourself blow a field of tall grass. Now you are blowing the clouds about. You blow farther and farther. You blow on the surface of the ocean, making waves rise and fall. You blow on and on. Now you are blowing far out into space. You blow on the sun and moon. You blow past the planets. Now you blow out to the stars. You blow on the stars and between the stars. You blow on and on forever.

Children's responses:

This meditation emerged spontaneously one windy afternoon. Both Stewart and Steve stated afterwards, "the wind sounds like waves crashing against the rocks."

MEDITATION ON CARING

On the blackboard of your mind see someone you care for. How does it feel to care for this person? Feel the feelings of caring you have in your heart for this person. How can you share this yummy feeling in your heart with more people? How can you care more for others? How can you show this caring for them? How can you care more for yourself, also? How can you show love more to yourself and to others? Send some love right now to someone who needs it. Send it to the whole world.

I lead this meditation slowly, with pauses between the questions to give time to answer the questions inside ourselves. Here are a few of the children's responses of how they could care more for themselves and others:

Do better in my work.

118

Not fight and hit.
Be kinder to others.
Start wearing warmer clothes.
Not to play jokes anymore.
Don't hurt other people, because then they won't hurt
you back.

FEATHER MEDITATION

*You are becoming a feather. Feel your softness. Feel how light
you are. The wind picks you up and you begin to float up and up, up
to the treetops. The wind carries you higher and higher. You are now
high above the treetops rising farther and farther up. You float up
into space beyond the earth, past the moon and sun—beyond the
planets. You float farther and farther. You float up to the stars. You
float past the stars. How far can you float? Can you find the end of the
universe? Now you begin to float back down to the earth. You feel
yourself floating down, down through space, past the stars, past the
planets, past the sun and the moon. The earth looks closer and closer
below you. You float down gently, farther and farther down until you
are passing up the treetops. Now you are gently landing on the earth.*

Children's responses:

One child felt herself shoot up to the stars then back to
the earth to land in a pond. Another child shared that a
raindrop took a ride on her as she was a feather. One child
was a red, white, and blue feather.

The children find this meditation very relaxing.

ROCK MEDITATION

*Feel you are a rock. What does it feel like to be a rock? Where are
you located? What kind of rock are you? Feel your surface. What are
you like inside? What color are you? Feel all the atoms and molecules
which make you up. Feel the atoms and molecules move within you.
Feel the energy inside yourself. Do you like being a rock?*

I did not record any children's responses to this
meditation.

JOY MEDITATION

Imagine a feeling of joy. You feel an opening in the top of your head. You feel joy floating down through the top of your head. It fills up your head and neck. It fills your shoulders and arms. The joy floats down into your chest, stomach and back. Now it is filling your abdomen and buttocks. It floats into your legs and feet. Every part of your body is full of joy. You are so full of joy, it begins to spread out beyond your body. It spreads out onto everyone in our classroom. It reaches out beyond the classroom farther and farther until it spreads over the whole earth. It continues to spread out even further into the universe—beyond the planets, beyond the stars, farther and farther. The whole universe is filled with joy.

Children's responses:

Tina became so relaxed from this meditation, she said she couldn't feel her eyes. The children enjoyed sending love to the whole world. Several children were able to feel the joy someone else in the class sent them.

LIZARD MEDITATION

You are becoming a lizard. What does it feel like to be a lizard? What color are you? What is your body like? What kind of lizard are ? How do you move around? How do you eat? How do you municate with other lizards? What do you do all day? What is it to be a lizard?

Children's responses:

The children enjoyed becoming a lizard. Bill shared afterwards that he was an iguana with no friends. So he shouted to the whole world real loud and then he had a lot of friends. Another boy shared that as a lizard he swallowed a magic fly. Then he saw a bird. Because he was now magic, he could blow himself up giant size and swallow the bird.

STAR OR CANDLE FLAME HELD IN THE CENTER OF THE FOREHEAD

Look up into the space between your eyebrows. See a star or a candle flame in that spot. Pay attention to your star or candle flame until I ring the little bell. (Teacher counts to 10, 20, 30 or more, depending on the children's age and ability to concentrate; then rings a soft bell.)

Children's responses to this meditation:

Some children experienced gold and silver stars, others rainbow colored ones. One child saw a star with candles coming out at each point. Tim saw a red candle which burned down. Then it turned orange.

Many of the children's stars or candle flames grew bigger, then smaller or vice versa. One child saw a star with a diamond in the center. Another felt a point on the top of her head.

Here are a few of the children's comments:

Bill—"My star got bigger and bigger. It burned my head. I could feel it."

Ellen—"I saw a star on an upside down candle. I counted to 19. Then it went away."

Alan—"My star is still burning."

WHITE-WINGED HORSE MEDITATION

(Roger asked if I would lead this meditation during the time when his mother was reading the story of Pegasus to him at night.)

Pretend that you are a white-winged horse. Feel yourself taking off in flight. Your wings are rising. You feel the air swishing against your wings. Now you are flying up and up, higher and higher. The trees and houses look small below you. You are flying over the city and beyond the city. You are flying over all the countries of the earth. You are flying farther and farther, on and on, past the earth. You are flying higher now. You rise up and up. You are flying past the moon and the sun, past the planets. Now you are flying way up amongst the stars.

Children's responses:

The children really liked this meditation and the ideas they shared would have made good stories.

UNDERWATER MEDITATION

(This meditation was made up spontaneously one hot October afternoon. The children were hot and asked to go under water during centering time.)

See the most beautiful waterfall you have ever imagined. A large pool of clear water lies under the waterfall. You dive into the pool, feeling the cool water touch your whole body. Feel the cool fresh water relaxing your head, your neck, your arms, back, chest, stomach, abdomen, legs and feet. Now you feel yourself dissolving and becoming the cool pool. You begin to spread out, cooling off the whole city. You spread even farther over the whole earth, cooling the earth. You feel totally refreshed.

Children's responses:

> Nearly half the class saw the waterfall and pool in rainbow colors. Others saw it in red, orange and pink colors. They really liked this meditation.

PLANT MEDITATION

You are a seed in the warm earth. You feel the soil all around you. You feel warm and safe in the soil. Warm rains are falling. You feel the warm rain fall on you. You drink up the rain and you begin to grow larger and larger. You begin to wiggle in the earth. You grow roots deep, deep into the soil. Your little stem grows up slowly until it begins to pop out of the soil. Your stem grows higher and higher up out of the soil. It grows taller and taller. Your roots grow deeper and deeper into the soil. You draw up water and food through your roots into your stem. Tiny branches begin to grow out from your stem. They spread out, growing larger and larger. Leaves begin to grow on your branches. Now your branches are covered with leaves. A flower bud begins to grow on top of your stem. It expands and grows larger and larger. Suddenly it bursts into full bloom. Now you are a beautiful flower. You reach up to the warm sun shining down on you—up and up you reach, closer and closer to the sun. You reach up farther and farther, growing towards the sun.

For younger children it is good to follow this meditation with a creative movement activity where the children act out the meditation with their bodies.

On the following page is one of the third-grade girls' responses to this meditation.

I was a seed and I was
in the store. One day a
lady came to the store
and bought me and she
planted me and I grew and
grew until I a rose.
More and more roses grew
on the bush and it was
pretty.

STORM MEDITATION
(Good to use during the stormy season)

Listen to the storm outside. Listen to the wind blowing against the building and blowing through the trees. Feel what the wind would feel like blowing on your face. Listen to the rain. Feel the wetness of the rain on your face. Now pretend that you are becoming the storm. You are the clouds moving very fast. You are the wind blowing the trees. You are the rain falling hard on the earth, the houses, and the streets. You are the lightning hitting the earth. What does it feel like to be a storm? Do you feel your power and energy? Feel yourself moving over the whole earth.

Children's responses:

> We did this meditation during a week when we were having tremendous storms. Eugene shared after this meditation that his lightning bolt split the earth into four pieces. Some children imagined they became raindrops and fell to the ground.

SUN MEDITATION

Imagine you are the sun. What does it feel like to be the sun? Feel your hotness and your fiery flames. How hot are you? Travel into your center. What is in the center of the sun? Hear the roaring sounds you make. Feel your light and energy radiating from your center outwards. Feel it radiating on the earth, warming it up, and on the planets. Feel it radiating farther and farther into space. You are shining on the other suns (stars in space). You shine on and on farther and farther. How far can you shine? Do you like being the sun?

I did not record the children's responses to this meditation.

HEART MEDITATION
(Good for Valentine's Day)

Pretend that you have a magic heart. Every time you put more love into the heart, it gets bigger and bigger. You fill your magic heart with love. It becomes so big, you fit inside it. You put more love into it and it grows yet bigger and bigger. It gets so big, the whole world is inside your heart, all the mountains, animals, oceans, plants and people are inside your heart. You put more love in it and it grows ever bigger. Now the whole universe is inside your magic heart, all the planets and stars, all of space is in your magic heart. Your magic heart is very big and filled with love.

Children's responses to the heart meditation:

Sandy—"My heart was a big monster and it had these other little hearts inside, and every time he would blow out these hearts it would make everyone happy."

Alan—"I sent little heart-shaped warm fuzzies filled with love to everybody in the classroom."

Mary—"I had a huge heart and I kept blowing it up and then when it got really huge, it popped, and it squirted love all over."

Rick—"My heart got bigger and bigger and then it got huge and it let out a whole lot of little hearts and they gave love to people. Then the heart came back inside me."

Tim—"I was God with a big heart and sent all the people love."

Don—"When my heart beat, it rumbled and the people thought it was an earthquake."

Bill—"I was a heart and ate the universe, all the people and all the stars. Then I blew up and everything started over again."

Brian—"When my heart was growing, I took a giant arrow and I shot it right through it and it squirted some love everywhere."

It takes cooperation to make a picture together.

CHAPTER 13

The Creative Flow

One thing I stumbled upon quite accidentally was the marvelous effect meditation had on children's art and creative writing. When and why I began to follow the morning meditations with a sequence of art and writing, I do not recall. At some time during the first year that I taught meditation to the children, I began to have the children draw or paint and then write, just after we had finished meditation. Perhaps I began to do this because so many beautiful images were emerging from the children's sharing after meditations and it just seemed natural to have the children express these images on paper.

It is only now in retrospect that I am becoming more aware of why the flow of events—meditation followed by art and writing—is so successful a flow for the children's expression. They are tuning into that inner voice, that inner creative voice we all have developed to some extent. Meditation seems to allow them to first discover their own inner voice and then to focus it. Art and writing immediately following meditation allow them to express, to bring out and make real in the world that private inner song.

For some of us our inner voice exists only as a chatter of thoughts which goes around and around in circles. Meditation allows the children to calm the normal chatter of the mind and tune to another part of themselves, that part wherein lies true imagination and true spontaneous creativity. Also in the type of meditation we were doing, we were drawing on many of the faculties of human consciousness. We were getting in touch with the emotions, releasing and then focusing them in a positive way. We were then concentrating the emotions, feelings and thoughts into one point and then expanding the focused consciousness through the intuition and imagination. Perhaps the children's art and writing is so creative and dynamic because meditation encourages the children to use so much more of their inner potential. The faculties of the emotions, the mind, the imagination and the intuition are all working together to help bring forward increased creativity and expression. Vibrant images of feelings lead to vibrant colors on the page, and children stretch their minds to come up with the words that can portray and clothe their inner experience.

Recently I heard Joseph Chilton Pearce speak of the way the aborigines stand on one foot and stare into space for a specific period of time. He encouraged teachers to allow students to do a similar type of staring. He explained how the children's natural urge to stare is their natural practice of meditation and how it helps keep their intellectual-creative system in balance with their outer environment.* Burton White, researcher at Harvard's Pre-School Project reported that the children who were the brightest, happiest and most charming had one characteristic in common:** they all spent as much as twenty percent of their time "staring" with total absorption at some object or another. These children, coming from a wide variety of backgrounds and experiences, spent more time "staring" than in any other single activity. Staring seems to be the small child's natural way to meditate and grasp knowledge of the world around him.

As a child I used to love to spend time in nature. I lived on a dairy and crop farm in the fertile Sacramento delta. I recall loving spring-time when the fruit trees in a small orchard would come into bloom. I would climb the trees and sit for hours in the branches, sometimes with eyes closed, listening intently to the sounds of the bees, sometimes with eyes open, staring at the beauty of the delicate

---

*Joseph Chilton Pearce's talk is written up in the Journal of Holistic Health, Volume VI, Del Mar, CA.: Mandala Holistic Health, 1981.
**Burton White, The First Three Years of Life,(Englewood Cliffs, N.J.: Prentice Hall, 1975.)

white and pink blossoms against a dark blue sky. Later, during the summer, I would again climb up into the branches of the trees, this time to stare at the sun dancing and creating multi-colored shades of green in the soft green leaves. What drew me almost daily to climb those trees and spend so much time in absorbed silence? What drew me also to spend so many evenings, walking in the sweet night air, finding a high place like a hay bale to sit or stand on to stare at a beautiful setting sun? And how often would I find myself breaking into spontaneous singing, making up songs to the whole universe before me exemplified in the fiery setting sun! Was I meditating? In thinking back to the feelings which arose in my heart as I communed with nature in those ways, I believe that I was indeed meditating in my own childlike unformed manner. Those moments were very soothing and quieting to my mind and being. Those were moments of great joy when my quieted mind would often soar away to think the deeper thoughts we all have about life—why am I here on this earth and what is this life all about? In these quiet moments my own inner dialogue was allowed to be and to express itself naturally. I continued all the way through high school to commune in this way with nature, relishing these precious moments, totally unconscious of what I was really doing.

But how is it possible for the children growing up in our busy, tense, anxious society to have these times of oneness, of inner nourishment for the soul? Children are often pushed aside to watch T.V. or fend for themselves. How many of them are given the space or are raised where their natural urge to "stare" or be quiet is encouraged? Perhaps this gives even more reason to bring to the classroom the deep inner experience meditation provides.

What I discovered was that drawing and writing after meditation developed the child's natural creativity in writing. I no longer had to provide a subject for the children to write about and prod them to think of ideas. And it certainly was difficult before I taught meditation to children to come up daily with subjects which all children would be interested in writing about. Now, through meditation, the children had their own rich world of images to draw and write from—images far more dynamic and creative than I could ever have provided. And the excitement that was generated for writing was coming from within themselves, not from me, so it did not take my energy to sustain it.

In having the children write daily after meditation I discovered something else: children's own creative writing is the best way to teach many of the basic grammar skills such as capitalization, punctuation, sentence structure, etc. These skills pointed out, looked at, corrected and taught through the children's own writing made the skills real for them. I put away the second- and third-grade English books which were full of exercises in which the children were to copy sentences and add, for instance, the proper form of "was" or "were" or the proper punctuation. Instead, I had each child look at the proper use of grammar and punctuation in his or her own writing. The children seemed to be learning these skills more quickly in this way and showed that they retained them by using them in future writing experiences.

I also began to notice that once I began to follow meditation with art and writing, the children's interest and ability to perform in other subject areas such as reading and math increased. They became extremely interested in vocabulary and tackling new words. Meditation made them happy. They were having a chance to get in touch daily with their own deep inner world and then express from that space. This seemed to carry over into all they did.

There is another reason why I believe that meditation stimulated the children to write. This was because the children were encouraged and given the opportunity to share verbally their images, perceptions and feelings following meditation. Many educators stress that writing is spoken language put down in writing and that children learn to write by practicing speaking and conversing. That is why many kindergarten and first-grade classrooms have the typical "show and tell" time. Verbal sharings following meditation became a very rich and dynamic "show and tell" time, if that name can even apply here. For the children were not just sharing their toys or what happened at their house last night but they were sharing feelings and perceptions full of rich imagery and expression. This is what carried over into their art and writing. It was very fulfilling to watch this unfoldment!

If we look at our society today, it seems we are not producing the quality of art, music and writing that we have seen rise and fall in past times, and there may be a good reason why. True potential and creativity may be stifled in our school system as it exists today. It may be time to open up the doors in our schools to what true education is all about.

For instance, I recall my teachers spending a lot of time teaching me nouns, verbs and parts of speech. I was a serious student and learned all that was put before me. But much of it did not stick. I have come away from the school system with an inadequate knowledge of English grammar and yet I was grilled in grammar many times. Why was it not retained? Perhaps because it was not taught in a way that had relevance to my life. We did not do much creative writing in school. We spent much of our time writing reports which were done by reading a textbook or encyclopedia and then re-expressing what we read in our own words. But we were given very little chance to express our inner worlds in a meaningful manner. So all those structured grammar lessons I had in school were essentially a waste of time. Far better had those skills been applied to my own writing. They would probably still be with me today.

As a teenager I also recall that my imagination was alive with images. I loved to ride in the car as my father drove the family because I loved to daydream. Actually what I did was make up stories, all kinds of stories in full vivid color and imagery. And in the same way, the children, following meditation, made up stories from their imaginations. Previous to teaching meditation, I would often have the children write an ending to a sentence I had written on the board. For instance, I may have written the following sentence, "I am glad that I can see." Then I would have encouraged the children to complete the thought. They may have written, "I am glad that I can see because I like to see my mom and I like to see flowers." Where was the child's true creative potential in this expression? Where was the heart and the imagination of the child? Following meditation, the child's heart and imagination flowed so naturally into a creative story all his own.

Here is a story written by Sonya, a quiet sweet second-grader. Note that it has a beginning, middle and ending.

You may be wondering why I was so delighted by a story like this written by a child. Perhaps this story seems simple to you. I was so pleased with stories like this which emerged from meditation because I had never had such young children do such delightful writing in my previous years of teaching. At the second-grade level I never stressed

Once upon a time a
little girl came out
to play. Then she saw
a little pupy was
trying to find it's way
home. The little girl
ran into her house.
She told her mother
all about the pupy. She
asked if she could keep
the pupy. So her
mother said, yes. She
ran out-side to get
the puppy. When she

was out t here the
puppy was gone.
The little girl cryed
and cryed and cryed.
Her mother came
out t here to see
what She was crying

about. Then She
knew what had
happend. Then
they fonud the
puppy.  The End.

that they include a beginning, middle and ending to a story, as they were often doing now spontaneously.

It was not uncommon for the second- and third-grade children, following meditation, to write a story the length of Sonya's. In recent work with children I had even had some first-graders write stories at least this long, following meditation. It takes a lot of discipline for young children to stay focused long enough to do this much writing on their own. Meditation had helped the children develop this quality of inner discipline and concentration. In my first years of teaching I felt fortunate when second-graders would write one page composed of two or three sentences. Now many are writing much more. You may note in Sonya's story that the word puppy is misspelled in the beginning of the story but spelled correctly towards the end. As she worked on the story I brought her attention to its correct spelling. By the end of the story she was beginning to spell the word correctly. I took the words each child misspelled in story writing and put them on cards which were then attached to a ring with the child's name on it. These words became the child's spelling words for the week. The children practiced them in many different ways during the week, often working in pairs. On Friday, a parent volunteer and I tested the children individually on the words on their rings. If they knew a word we cut the card. It became an exciting way to teach spelling. The children loved it, some children challenging themselves to learn up to thirty words per week.

One year the children became very interested in some books which came out on the market about gnomes, little elf-like creatures with pointed hats. Because of the high interest in gnomes, I led the children in several meditations which included a guided fantasy about gnomes. The children simply couldn't wait to share the images which came up in their imaginations afterwards. They were very motivated to write, following these meditations.

Sandy, a dynamic spunky third-grade girl with dark brown hair and dark brown eyes, wrote the following story. She stayed fully absorbed in the writing of it for at least thirty minutes.

You may note again the length of the story, which is long for a third-grader. You may also note that Sandy used punctuation well.

I was a giant and I
lived in a castle and
I just woke up from my
nap and I wanted to
get fresh air. So I went
out side for a little bit.
And then I saw some little
people and I didn't know
they were gnomes and they
didn't like big people.
They were playing a game of
some sort. I liked plaing
games so I asked them if
I coued play with them
but they ran away from
me. I was rully sad.

I went home and did centering and it made me feel better. So then I tried agien and found them and they came to me and asked me if they coued play on me and I said yes and we became friends and we played together. So then they shoed me there house but I didn't like it so I said I woued make then a new one and they said ok.

The End

She had gained this skill through daily writing practice.

Many of the children were motivated, as Sandy was, to write long stories in response to the gnome meditation. Here is a gnome story by Roberta, a sweet gentle third-grader.

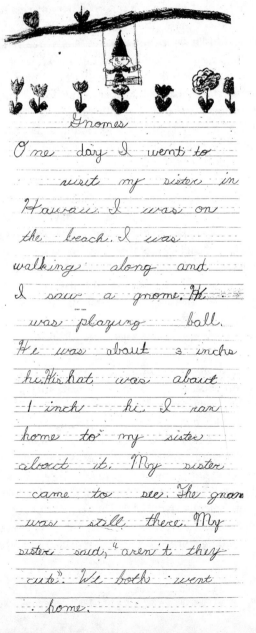

Gnomes

One day I went to visit my sister in Hawaii. I was on the beach. I was walking along and I saw a gnome. He was playing ball. He was about 3 inches hi. His hat was about 1 inch hi. I ran home to my sister about it. My sister came to see. The gnome was still there. My sister said, "aren't they cute". We both went home.

Note Roberta's proper use of capitals and periods. I have always found this skill difficult to teach primary age children. They often write wonderful stories, totally leaving out capitals and periods. Now through daily writing, the majority of the students began to use capitals and periods correctly most of the time. If children were having difficulty with this skill, I would sit down with them, one at a time, and have them read me their story. Then I would say, "Let's put the capitals and periods in where you need to take a breath. That's usually where they go. You start reading and tell me where the first period should go." In this way the children learned this important skill naturally through their own work. It took a little extra time to work with the children in this way but the results made it well worth the extra time. I often had a parent volunteer work in the classroom as we did the writing so that more children could be reached individually in this way.

You may note that Roberta used quotation marks in her story. This was a language skill she did not know. I worked with her and explained to her that the "talking parts" of a story, the parts where people talk, have special marks, called quotation marks, around them. I had her find the "talking part" in her story herself and then showed her how to use the marks. I found that by showing the children how to use quotation marks two or three times while having them identify the "talking parts" in their stories themselves, they were from then on usually able to use quotation marks correctly.

Shawn, a third-grade boy who had considerable pain in his life, in spite of his young age, often got in touch with images in meditation which seemed to add some security to his life. In his outward actions Shawn often acted in a manner which caused others to reject him, but in his inner world Shawn was a deeply sensitive and caring person. In his sharings after meditation, Shawn often shared this more vulnerable part of himself, and began to express these deeper qualities in his story writing as well. Note the sensitive caring exemplified in Shawn's gnome story and picture. Note also Shawn's use of cursive writing.* The children had learned cursive writing only a few months before they wrote the gnome stories. Because of the daily writing of their own

---

*Cursive writing is adult style handwriting in which the child learns to blend the letters together.

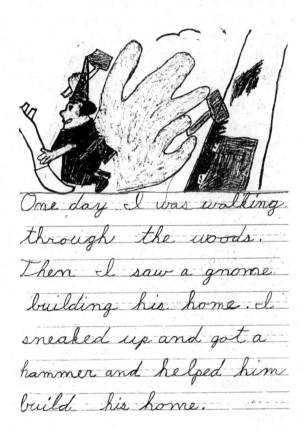

One day I was walking through the woods. Then I saw a gnome building his home. I sneaked up and got a hammer and helped him build his home.

stories, they had quickly become proficient in cursive writing. Shawn used complete sentences in his story. I found that the children seldom wrote run-on sentences and incomplete sentences. It was wonderful to watch them grow in these skills.

Following a meditation the children would often capture a wonderful sense of adventure in their stories. Don, while still in second grade, wrote a story especially full of adventure with an ending which I just love. This story was written following the spaceship meditation from *Meditating With Children*.

140

Adventure on Alligator Planet

I went up to a planet. I crashed and monsters came out
of the planet. They fixed my spaceship and sent me off to
another planet. Then I crashed again, this time on a Pink
Panther planet. Then they turned me into an alligator and
fixed my spaceship and sent me off. I crashed into a planet
of alligators. The alligators came out. They lost their baby
alligator and they thought I was their baby alligator, so they
kept me up there and I'm still there.*

Don wrote this story in response to being led in a meditation in
which he went in a spaceship which went out into outerspace farther
and farther in every direction, looking for the end of the universe.

Some of the children's stories following meditation reminded me of
the fables from the past. Here is just such a story written by Tammie, a
sweet, quiet third-grade girl. It could have been titled, "How I Learned
to Jump." Tammie was one of the children who was not a strong
imager but lived more in the world of feelings. Feelings are woven into
her story, motivating the character of her story to change. In this story,
Tammie was probably talking about her own inner world and what
really motivated her to change.

"I was a rabbit and I didn't know how to jump. I saw all
the other rabbits jumping. And I was just standing there. I
was embarrassed. Then some rabbits came over and made
fun of me, 'You don't know how to jump?' They kept saying
it and I got so mad I started to jump and that's how I know
how to jump."

Remember Anthony, age eight, the boy who learned how to hold
his own center so as not to care if he was called names on the
playground? When thinking of him, I often recall his wonderful stories
about Snoopy. As Anthony's imagination opened up in meditation, so
did a marvelous potential for writing. His inner world was chock-full of
powerful images, and before the end of the year he was writing some
wonderful stories. Here is one he wrote at Christmas time. Note the
warmth he expressed in this story. This warmth was very revealing of
Anthony's true nature; it often shone out of his eyes.

---

*The first and second years I taught meditation to children I transcribed the children's
stories in my journal. This is one of the stories I recorded in my journal. The third year I
decided to actually keep some of the children's work so that their pictures and
handwriting could appear in this book.

Snoopy's Christmas

One Christmas Snoopy wished he could have a puppy and finally Christmas came and Snoopy looked in a box and a light brown puppy was jumping on Snoopy. Snoopy was so happy. He did love the little puppy. Two years later the puppy had children and Snoopy was so proud. The puppy had babies and Snoopy said we have to get a Christmas tree and we will celebrate Christmas with the puppies.

The wonderful thing about Anthony's writing was that he had been labeled educationally handicapped and was now breaking out of that label into his own true creative potential. It was very exciting to see the confidence he was gaining through this type of experience.

Alan, also age eight, wasn't labeled educationally handicapped as Anthony was, but you may recall how he encountered much difficulty learning because he couldn't concentrate. You may also recall that his ability to focus and concentrate improved through daily participation in meditation and so did his academic work. Alan began to write longer and longer stories. It was such a delight to watch him change. At the beginning of the year, all he could do was write a few garbled unreadable words on a piece of paper. Now he could write a complete story, a story fun for others to read and experience. He began to enjoy his newly-found skill with his classmates. Here is a story which he wrote at Easter time.

One day rabbit was walking in the meadow and saw a butterfly. He wanted to catch it so he ran after it.

When the butterfly stopped it landed on the roof of an evil villain's house, and the rabbit went in.

The evil villain heard something and he hid on the other side of the door. When rabbit walked in, he jumped out in front of him and put him in a bag.

The evil villain had not eaten in months and he decided to eat the little rabbit for dinner. He put the little rabbit in boiling hot water, but the little rabbit was lucky because the pot had been burned so often that a hole had been made in the bottom.

He blew out the fire to escape, then climbed out and went through a little hole in the bottom of the floor.

He got out from the basement window and went home

to his mother and told of his exciting adventure.

He had to hurry because Easter was coming and he had to color the eggs.

He filled up each Easter basket with candies, colorful eggs and stuffed *toy* rabbits for all the kids.

He delivered each basket quickly before Easter so he could get to each house.

Finally, Easter was over and he went home again for a nap.

When he woke up it was winter all over again and he had to hibernate until next Easter.

THE END

Following meditation, sometimes the child's inner imagination expresses itself on paper in an unformed flowing manner. This type of writing is similar to the "stream of consciousness" writing of James Joyce. Such writing of children may not make a lot of sense to us, but it has deep psychological meaning to the child. I believe that it is very important for children to express this part of themselves in writing, if they can, as writing helps the children to understand these images and relate them to their lives. Tim, one of the eight-year-old boys in the class, had a series of similar images occur each morning for a whole week during our morning meditation centering time. Each day a new adventure came to him which added to the original image. Each morning he wrote down what he experienced during the meditations. He divided what he wrote into three chapters. After his writing was complete, he drew a picture to go with it. Here is what Tim drew and wrote:

Tim's Story

Chapter 1

Once upon a time there was a flea. He was in a guy's ear doing centering. All of a sudden there was a wax slide. The flea woke up and hid behind another hunk of wax. The next day they had to clean out the guy's ear. They poured some baby oil in the guy's ear. The poor flea practically drowned but that was his water fall. That day he had school. His classroom was all hair. His stage had a drum. The flea played the drum all the time. Once he had a concert. It was great. Everybody loved it.

Chapter 2

One year later the flea went up to the guy's eye. The guy scratched his eye. It was like a trampolin to the flea and it was practically midnight. The guy was asleep. The flea met another flea. The little flea poured a bucket of water and woke the guy up. The other flea told him to dry the guy's eyelashes. The other flea did it with a part of brain. The little flea did centering again. He imagined there was a candle. There was a candle. The two fleas picked up the candle and walked along while they were wabling along.

Chapter 3

One year later one of the fleas went up to the guy's head. It was like a forest to the flea. He chopped down all the trees which were hairs. Pretty soon the guy was bald. The guy had a dinner date that night. The guy was bald. What should he do. He put on a wig. That night the flea had a fire. The wig burned up. The lady looked at the man. She screamed and ran away. So did the flea.

THE END

The Flea

You can tell that Tim's writing is a flow of consciousness because he keeps weaving in thoughts and feelings about the centering process itself. When he refers to the waterfall he is identifying with the centering process because I sometimes had the children imagine a waterfall of light splashing over their bodies during the first part of the meditation to help them relax. The image of the candle also came from the centering process, as we often focused on a candle flame in the center of the forehead for concentration. I found it interesting that Tim wove thoughts about the centering process into a story which emerged from the centering process itself. Somehow I feel that the flea was actually Tim in disguise, the same way that each character in our dreams is actually a different aspect of our own consciousness, and that this story had deep meaning for him. This story was left in its original form. Tim could have been encouraged to take this stream of consciousness and turn it into a more polished product. I did not, however, encourage him to change it.

The flow of events—meditation followed by art and writing—proved to have additional benefits for the children. One was an increase in the ability to read. One of my second-grade girls actually learned to read, more because of her daily writing than because of reading skill lessons. Each morning, following meditation, she would with utmost care, write about three sentences to go with a colorful picture she had drawn. She would then read the three sentences softly over and over to herself. She did this daily, often choosing to stay in and spend part of her recess time reading her story. I observed a marked improvement in her reading progress not long after she began to do this.

During the first year that I taught meditation to children, I attended a language arts workshop. In the workshop it was suggested that teachers have children write their own reading books, writing and illustrating them themselves. I began to have the children write such books on certain mornings, following meditation. The children loved writing their own books after meditation. Some children spent a long time on one book, making it anywhere from twenty to forty pages long. As each child's book was finished, it went into a special place in our classroom library, so that the rest of the class could read it during free reading time. These little books became the children's favorite reading books. Here are the pages of one of the books written by a six-

and-a-half year-old during his first month in second grade. He titled it "The Man and the Creature".

This ship is taking-off.

1

This ship is off and away.

2

The rocket landed on Mars.

3

Then the man walked around.

4

Then The man saw a creature.

5

Then They made friends.

6

The children also kept journals and were free to write in their journals whatever they wished. I did not, as some teachers do, read the journals. At the end of the last year that I taught meditation in the public schools, some of the children allowed me to take their journals home so that I could photocopy them to be included in this book. The children usually wrote less in their journals than they wrote when they did creative writing in the morning, because I only gave them ten minutes to write in their journals as opposed to a half hour to forty-five minutes for story writing in the morning. Sometimes the children chose to write in their journals about their experiences in meditation. Here are several recordings in journals from two different children in response to a meditation in which we imagined we were the sun shining farther and farther out to the whole universe.

Today In my mind the sun shined out of my head and every body In the school came runing to the class room.

When I was tha sun I
had a lot of freinds.
AND I had a lot of colors.
When every morning
came I would go out and
wake every person
up.

Here is a page from Bill's journal when he was in second grade. This was in response to the spaceship meditation from *Meditating With Children*, in which we tried to find the end of the universe. His representation of a force field is simply delightful.

I Found the end of the universe I Blasted the 8 force field.

Another second-grader recorded in this manner her response to the earth meditation from the same book:

I'm the earth and eury body walks on me I love eury body on the earth.

Sometimes the children wrote in their journals about the things which gave them joy. Here is one such recording:

I feel Happy
because I
Get to ride
my bike home
with my Sister
and John.

At other times they recorded their unhappy feelings.

Sep 21, 1978

I felt mad because I had a headache.

Sometimes the children recorded feelings of concern about their friends. Bill found his friend Louis sitting on the bench one lunch recess. Louis was sitting on the bench because he had disobeyed one of the school rules during the lunch hour. Bill recorded in his journal:

I Felt Bad Because I Found Louis Sitting on the bench.

I believe writing in their journals following meditation worked well for the children because the time in meditation gave the children a chance to really tune into how they were feeling before they were encouraged to express their feelings. The children took pride in keeping their journals and kept them very neat.

Most children love to paint and draw. Each morning I had the children draw or paint a picture, either just before they did their writing or immediately afterwards. They also loved drawing pictures in their journals.

They usually could hardly wait to sit down and draw and paint the feelings and images which emerged from meditation. They were usually disappointed on mornings when there was no time to draw. Sometimes their drawings were full of humor. One morning we imagined we were baby elephants during meditation. All the children were asked to draw what they experienced during the meditation. Here is what I recorded in my journal about their drawings: "The pictures the children drew afterwards were fantastic. Tim drew a baby elephant in a diaper—with a giant safety pin and all. Joseph drew an elephant baseball player. The children wanted to put their pictures up on the wall so their parents could see them at Back to School Night. There was no wall space available so we put them on the windows. They were a great hit!"

Once a friend of mine visited the class and participated in the meditation with us. Afterwards his eyes sparkled just like many children's do following meditation. After the meditation I gave the children large pieces of drawing paper and sent them to their seats to draw. My friend came up to me and said, "Now I know why you have the children meditate before you have them draw! I saw a picture in my mind of a white dove, as you led the meditation, and I can hardly wait to draw it. I remember when I was in school I never knew what to draw when the teacher asked us to draw. This makes it so easy."

I went to the Holistic Education Conference in San Diego several summers ago. In one of the workshops, the instructor led us in a meditation. Afterwards she had us draw and write some sentences about our drawings. I drew some mountains with snow caps on them and a cave below. The whole process was a very fulfilling experience. Now I knew from going through the process myself, why drawing and writing following meditation was such a fulfilling experience for the children. It deepened my belief in this method of teaching.

Early on in my student teaching days I took a class in children's art. We learned how younger children tend to draw isolated symbols on a page. They may draw, for instance, the sun up in one corner, the grass below and a flower in the middle of their picture. We learned that children do not start to fill in the whole page of a drawing, giving their symbols a background, until they are about ten years old. After participating in meditation for awhile and drawing daily, following meditation, to my surprise some of the children began to fill in the whole page. First one child began drawing in this manner, then another and another. It was quite amazing to watch the unfolding of this newly-found skill. They were not copying from one another, either, but just naturally seemed to add more and more background to their pictures. Following are a few examples of pictures eight-year-old children drew where they filled in the whole page:

Here is an entry in one eight-year-old boy's journal in which he filled in the whole picture, adding some background. Note the delicately drawn bee and the interesting way this boy drew vines growing up on a tree.

Other children began to do overlay in their drawings—in other words, they drew a picture and then drew another part of the picture over what they had already drawn. On the next page is one of the third-grade girls' pictures. First she drew the streets and houses. Then she drew a rainbow right over them. I had never had a child this age draw overlay in this way before.

As a result of meditation, the children's ability to concentrate and draw in intricate detail increased, as exemplified in this picture of a butterfly drawn by a third-grade girl. The children would stay absorbed in intricate drawings like this one for long periods of time, following a meditation.

Here is another picture drawn in fine pencil work by a third-grade boy named Terry. Note the tiny bird in the nest. He tended to be clumsy and it was surprising to see him begin to draw in this not only detailed but very sensitive manner. He usually kept this more sensitive part of himself somewhat hidden.

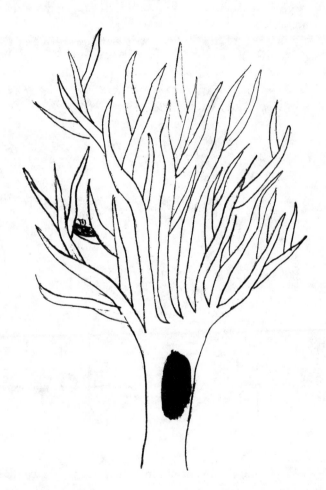

I noted that the children did more detailed work in art and craft projects as well. In my journal on February 6, 1978, I wrote, "The children did a more intricate job on their Valentine and snowflake art projects this year than my third-grade classes have ever done before. They have finer motor control."

Remember Brian, the third-grade boy who made a tape of meditation to play for himself at home and whose concentration improved as soon as he learned to keep his body still in meditation? He drew this picture one morning. He worked quietly on it for a full forty-five minutes, carefully adding each flower. How wonderful it was to see him draw with such concentration! He had never done anything like this before.

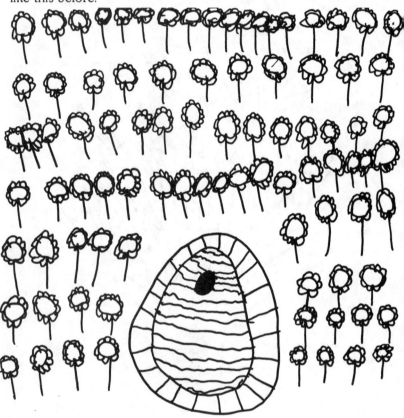

Another thing my eight-year-old students began to do was to draw in perspective in a way not normally seen in this age child. They began to draw in this more mature manner totally on their own, with no instruction from me. It seemed to emerge naturally from their experience of meditating and drawing daily. The sample drawings on the following page show the norm for each age group:

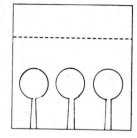

Children younger than eight years old show perspective by using the bottom of the paper as a baseline and arrange all forms on the line in vertical position. They show the sky as a narrow horizontal plane across the top of the page.

Between the ages of eight and nine years old children begin to show simple perspective by placing their figures, animals, houses and trees on two or more baselines which cross the paper horizontally and are arranged one above the other.

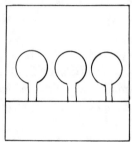
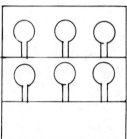

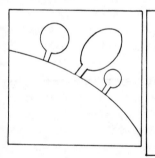
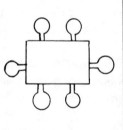

To show trees or a hillside or houses on a city block in perspective eight- and nine-year-old children use the line of the hill or the squared-up line of the city block as the baseline and arrange figures on those baselines in positions perpendicular to the lines.

Between the ages of nine and eleven children begin to show perspective by scattering their figures, animals and trees on the page, being careful not to let them touch or overlap, and they place short horizontal baselines under each figure. They begin to show distance by drawing the nearest objects large and drawing them low on the paper.

You can see an example of how eight-year-old children show perspective by drawing several baselines, by turning to page 157. Here the child has drawn two streets as two different baselines, one on top of the other. Eight-year-old Rochelle, who drew this picture, placed houses on both baselines.

After drawing every morning following meditation, many of the children eight years old began to no longer use baselines in this manner to show perspective but began to use perspective in a much more sophisticated fashion.

On the next page you will find eight-year-old Sandy's drawing. Here Sandy draws the hills going back in perspective, one hill in back of the other, each hill smaller than the one before. The winding brown road shows a mature use of perspective as it grows smaller and smaller in the distance. Sandy does not place her trees on baselines at all. (Even nine- to eleven-year-olds often still use baselines). Sandy shows perspective by drawing the trees smaller and smaller on the receding hills. The two tiny trees on the left have a hammock between them, drawn very delicately, looking much like the hammock between the two trees in the front center of the picture. You can see a reflection in the river of the birds from the sky. This reflection is drawn below the trees. Sandy's use of perspective is very unusual for an eight-year-old.

On page 155 you can see a second example, similar to Sandy's, of how some of the students began to use perspective in their rendering of hills and mountains by drawing one hill in back of the other.

An eight-year-old boy uses perspective in a very sophisticated manner on page 164. Again recall the way an eight-year-old normally uses perspective by placing objects on horizontal baselines placed on top of one another to show that the objects go back in space and how they do *not* use diagonals to show this.* In this picture we see diagonals used to show the truck moving up the hill, into space.

---

*In Heinrich Wölfflin's book, *Principles of Art History* (New York: Dover Publications, Inc., 1950), the author explains how this difference in the rendering of space is unfolded in evolution of Western art—the "plane" method used up through the 16th century, then giving way in the 17th century to the "recessional" method, when artists discovered how to create perspective by diagonals.

Note also the use of perspective in the truck bed and in the rendering of the unfinished roof on the building. Even the little stubs of chopped-down trees show an advanced use of perspective in the way the circular tops are drawn.

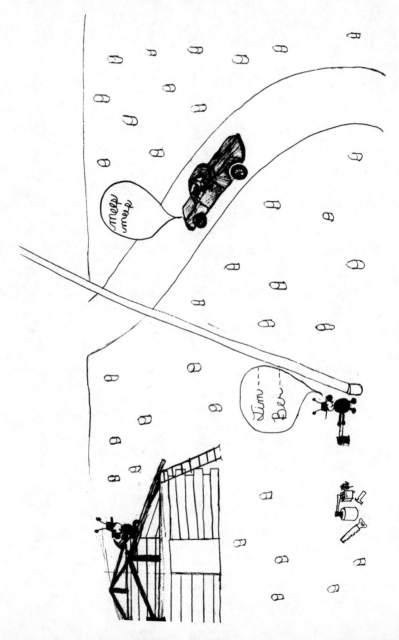

Children normally don't become interested in discovering more mature ways of showing perspective, overlapping and shading until the junior high level, between the ages of eleven and fourteen. What had caused my eight-year-olds to begin to tackle more difficult approaches to perspective? Could it be that meditation was opening the children up to more and more of their potential?

I believe all children deserve the opportunity to get in touch with and learn to express themselves in the way these children had the chance to do and to be encouraged by their peers, parents and teachers. What better way to learn than through one's own inner source of creativity, with learning drawn from the inside out? Meditation proved to be a marvelous way to make this happen.

The author guides the child to appreciate the sense of touch and how a flower really feels.

CHAPTER 14

Awareness Games

After a meditation, children have a heightened, dynamic energy that is just waiting to be used. Failing to do something with it is like opening a door to the child's potential without realizing what a precious gift it really is. Both art and creative writing are natural ways of expressing this energy. Science experiments, discussion, creative movement and dance are also wonderful ways to use this energy. But in my experience, the most profound way to direct the children's energy, built up in meditation, is to have them participate in awareness games from *Exploring Inner Space*, a book written by Christopher Hills and Deborah Rozman. These games are also the most fulfilling way, because the children enjoy them so much. I have never seen such vibrant joyful expressions on children's faces as I invariably see during and immediately following an awareness game.

I had been teaching meditation for a year before I discovered the awareness games, and the children loved them from the start. In fact, they liked them so much, they didn't ever want the games to end. They were especially fond of the awareness games in which they used their intuitions. Their favorite activity was to sit knee to knee and send messages to one another from one mind to another silently, then checking after a few minutes to see if the other person received the message which was sent. They liked to do this activity both with eyes open and eyes closed. In this exercise it is customary for the child who is going to send a message to the other, to grasp the wrist of the other child. This sender visualizes something which has meaning for him. An animal, a spaceship, or a toy are all examples of things the children enjoyed sending to one another. The receiver tries to stay open and receptive like a photographic plate to receive the message from the sender. The children then switch roles and the receiver becomes the sender and the sender the receiver. Afterwards the children share whether they received one another's messages or not.

We did this exercise early in September the third year I taught meditation to the children. The children asked to keep their eyes open during the exercise. They took the exercise quite seriously, especially those who had been in my class the year before and had previous experience with it. Only a few children giggled. It's a bit hard at first for children not to giggle in exercises when they look into one another's eyes. It even became difficult for me not to burst into laughter as I watched the children, noticing how funny they looked being so serious and staring so intently into one another's eyes. I found myself turning to look the other way a few times and biting my tongue to keep from laughing. Afterwards the children shared what they received from their partners. Many children accurately received what their partner had sent. They became quite excited when they discovered they received one another's messages. Some even began to jump up and down with joy. Wide-eyed expressions and jubilant grins filled the room.

I found that the children, especially after meditating for a few months, became very good at receiving one another's messages. The whole class was soon able to send and receive messages with about 80% accuracy. Some of the children became very close friends because of the exercise. Many of these children liked to do the exercise time and again with a person they had grown close to through it. Tim and Don, two boys who became close in this way, became very good friends by the end of the year.

I usually participated with the children in the awareness games. It wasn't as easy for me to receive messages as it was for the children. In fact, during the first two years of teaching meditation to the children I did not pick up a single message the children sent me! It was sometimes frustrating, seeing the children being so successful at using their intuitions and feeling I was not able to participate fully. Then one

"That's it! Exactly what I was thinking!"

January afternoon, I received a message for the first time from a large dark-haired third-grader who was new to the school. Her name was Joannie. She had been in the class only a few months. She had come to the school because her foster family of eight years decided they didn't want her anymore, so she was being adopted by a local family. Joannie was going through a time of adjustment and was often very moody, so I hadn't really gotten too close to her up until the time that we did the exercise. We sat down knee to knee to send messages to one another. A special feeling of real joy and warmth flowed between us as we began the exercise. Joannie wanted me to send a message first, which I did. Then she sent her message, and afterwards we shared what we each picked up. She had picked up a red rose which I had sent her and I picked up little yellow chicks which she had sent me. We both laughed with joy. The air between us tingled. Now I knew why the children became so excited when they picked up one another's message and why they felt so close. Before the school year ended, Joannie returned to her original foster family. I was sad to see her go. We had developed a nice rapport.

A few weeks later I was again successful in picking up a message. This time my partner was Jack, a very sensitive boy who hid his sensitivity by complaining a lot and making it difficult for others, including myself, to feel close to him. He picked up the red roses I sent him. I picked up the football he sent me. We both felt exhilarated and felt a warm close vibration both during and after the exercise. I continued to feel closer to Jack after that.

Some of the children made up games of their own using the intuition, after participating in the activity a few times. A group of girls liked to form a circle at lunch time on rainy days in a corner of the room, and play a game where one girl started a message. She sent it to the next girl in the circle in silence, who sent it to the girl next in the circle in silence, and so on until the message had been passed from one mind to the other back to the person who started it, without a word being spoken. Then they checked to see if it had gotten around the circle correctly. They were very excited when they found they could indeed send the message correctly around the circle without words. The girls would often stay absorbed in the game the whole lunch hour.

As you can see, grounding the children's energies through the awareness games from *Exploring Inner Space* became a very fulfilling experience. The games certainly expanded the scope and dimension of my curriculum. Up to this time, only three levels of human potential were emphasized in the children's day in the school where I taught. They included mostly the intellect and to some extent social aware-ness and the physical body and senses. The games from *Exploring Inner Space* stimulated and opened the students to a much wider range of their inherent potential, including seven levels of conscious-ness in all: imagination, intuition, conceptualization and memory, emotions (life force and energy), intellect, social awareness and the physical body with its senses. These doorways to true human potential are present in all children and adults, but not everyone develops or uses them in exactly the same way. Some levels may be developed more than others in an individual. No level is better than another. To be a truly balanced and fulfilled person we need to have all seven levels functioning in our lives.

One of the purposes of the book on awareness games is to help people become closer to one another as they grow to understand that human beings act and function from these many different levels of consciousness. If I, for instance, am not a person who functions mostly from the physical level of consciousness, but I understand that there are people who do and I understand what their behavior is like, then I become more capable of accepting a person who functions from the physical level, instead of feeling that he or she should be more like me.

In those early years I made a basic assumption that the children in my class were too young to consciously understand the levels in this way. I have more recently discovered in my work with children that this is not true. Young children can use and understand the levels. I did find, however, as in the case of Jack and myself, that the awareness games automatically helped the children drop barriers and become closer to one another, whether they understood the process or not.

Laura and Anna were two girls who grew closer to one another through the awareness games. Laura related to life a lot from the intellectual level of consciousness, very curious to understand how and why things worked. She took pride in her school work, spending much time perfecting her academic skills. Anna related to life more in a social way (the social level of consciousness). Her main concerns were her friends, how they were feeling and how she was getting along with them. Not having someone to play with bothered her a lot, whereas Laura was not so concerned with whether or not she had friends and was quite content to spend long periods of time by herself. This is not to say that Laura did not have friends but that this was not something she put great emphasis on. Laura and Anna, although they did not dislike one another, did not choose one another as friends in the class. One afternoon, however, they were partners in the message sending and receiving awareness game. Looking at the sensitive expressions on their faces during the game, I could tell that they had bonded with one another on a new level—the level of the heart. Laura and Anna began to play together more often following the awareness game and whenever they interacted in class, they related with a new-found sensitivity and caring. It was beautiful to experience.

Sending and receiving.

Another game the children enjoyed was sensing color through their hands and bodies. The purpose of the exercise was to begin to see how different colors affect us. We began the awareness game with a meditation in which we imagined we were surrounded by and breathing in each of the colors of the rainbow. Then the children closed their eyes while I held up different colors of construction paper. The children were to see if they could sense or feel what color I was holding up. The children began to hold up their hands to see if they could sense the color through their hands. They expressed feeling warm or cold sensations from different colors. Stewart, a serious dark-haired boy in the class, saw and smelled different images in his imagination as I held up each color of construction paper. With his eyes tightly closed when the color green was held up he said, "I smell a forest." For yellow he said, "I smell a lemon." His responses were so spontaneous. His eyes sparkled afterwards when he saw how each image matched the color which was shown. The children had great fun with this activity and stayed fully absorbed in it for a full forty-five minutes, a long time for seven-year-old children to stay focused. They didn't want to stop it either, when it was time for lunch.

In introducing the awareness games in the public school system, I knew that I was teaching something totally new to that system. Therefore I introduced the games gradually, adding a few new ones every few weeks. At Back to School Night I showed pictures of the children doing the awareness games and explained them to the parents to help educate the parents about their value. Now I would include the awareness games in any curriculum I was providing, not only because I believe in them, but also because the children love them!

Resolving conflict makes us closer.

CHAPTER 15

Creative Conflict in the Classroom

Another process I discovered through Deborah Rozman and brought to my children was Creative Conflict, a method of communication which helps resolve conflict and builds bonds of trust. It worked very well in the classroom and I have never found a better way of resolving fights. The following chapter is about Creative Conflict and the marvelous effects it had on the children.

Conflict has always been part of our children's lives. How often do we see fights and conflicts arise between children out on the school playground, at lunch time or in the middle of a game? How often do conflicts arise over and over again, between the same children? How often do teachers go home feeling exhausted and drained because of all the conflicts we have had to help resolve during the day? I recall the times that I felt I just couldn't deal with one more fight. At times it seemed like I was spending half my time teaching and half my time resolving conflicts or disciplining students. I often pondered on this late at night, wondering why a teacher could not spend more time teaching.

Conflict seems to be on the rise in our schools now that children are coming to us with increasing internal pain to deal with. I sometimes think back to the year when I taught as a student teacher in a school where children threatened teachers and fellow students with knives and other weapons. I recall teaching a reading lesson to a group of children who kicked one another under the table with anger which seemed to be coming from some place deep inside themselves which had nothing to do with the classroom, anger so pent-up and frustrated that it lashed out at the closest person in sight. This anger was coming from some of the quietest, most withdrawn children in the class. It was impossible to really teach these children in the state of consciousness they were in, and they struggled along in the lowest reading group. It pained me to see the children in this state and I felt helpless to really effectively deal with them, not having the skill or training to deal with deep psychological problems. Nor did their classroom teacher know how. She was a warm dynamic woman, who struggled constantly to maintain strict discipline over the children. She did not seem to have either the time or know-how to deal with the pain and conflict which seethed and bubbled under the surface maintained by this discipline. We went on teaching the three R's, as though none of this inner conflict were happening.

Lately there has been a lot of emphasis on getting *back* to the three R's, but in the ten years I worked in the public school system I did not find that we stopped teaching them. Quite the opposite seemed to be happening in fact; we kept looking for better and more effective ways to teach the three R's. What seemed to be blocking learning was that children were coming to school less able to learn. I felt more and more like I was becoming not a teacher but a great gladiator keeping all the wild bulls from tearing the classroom and one another apart.

Creative Conflict is a communication process which helps a person deal with and confront conflict head-on. This method was developed by Christopher Hills and was being used successfully for adults at the University of the Trees in Boulder Creek, California. I began to take my first Creative Conflict class for adults at the University of the Trees in January 1977, just after I finished an awareness class with Deborah Rozman. At first I was just learning the process myself and did not see how it could be applied to children. But during the second year, I began to gradually use some of the simple steps with the students as conflicts arose. I was slow to bring it to children because I did not feel I could teach them something I did not understand well myself.

Creative Conflict is designed to penetrate basic ego separations between individuals. It can be a very deep and moving experience with adults and children alike. It begins with trust and open sharing. The first year I introduced Creative Conflict to my students they had already built up a sense of trust and caring through meditation and the awareness games. Creative Conflict seemed like a logical step to help them resolve conflicts. Meditation and Creative Conflict seemed to go hand in hand and we often meditated before a Creative Conflict.

The Creative Conflict process has a series of seven steps which lead to deeper and deeper communication. They include the centering meditation, receptivity, active listening, mirroring, confirmation, response, and confirmation again. Whenever children came in from recess fighting, I first had them sit down to do a centering meditation with lots of rhythmic breathing to release built-up tension and feelings. This would often release some of the anger or hurt the children were feeling and put them in a more receptive state to listen to one another. I then allowed one child, usually the most disturbed chlid, to speak first. He was encouraged to speak with "I-messages" and express feelings such as, "I felt angry when you kicked me out of the game because I felt lonely and left out." Usually it takes gentle encouragement and a few questions on my part before all the feelings are out. To draw a child out more, I would say, "And how did that make you feel?" The other child he was conflicting with was encouraged to become receptive and actively listen to the speaker. This was not always easy for a child to do; he sometimes interrupted the speaker, wanting to put his two cents in. I had to remind him that he would get his turn later to speak, once he had really heard the speaker. After the speaker had finished, then the other child was asked to mirror back what the speaker had said.

Mirroring is an extension of active listening. In mirroring you not only mirror back to a person what they have just said to you but you try to mirror the feelings and vibration of the person, what the person is saying behind their words. You try to experience the person as they are experiencing themselves. After mirroring comes confirmation. I would ask the first speaker to express whether he felt the mirror was accurate or not, whether he felt the child or children who listened to him understood him. If he said, "Yes", then this was confirmation. Then it was time for the other child to express his feelings. But if the speaker said, "No, that's not what I meant," then I asked him to express his feelings again. The other child was asked to listen and mirror again. We did this until the first child had been fully heard and understood.

Now it was time for the other child to respond. He was asked to share what he felt about what the speaker had just said. He too was encouraged to speak from "I messages". After he communicated, then the first speaker who had now become the listener was asked to mirror back what the second speaker had just communicated. If he had not heard, that child would speak again. This continued until he showed in his mirror that he fully understood the other.

I have found that the process of having the children express real feelings and having them mirror one another, often resolves a conflict very quickly. You can actually feel the tension and anger leave the room as they express themselves. Often fights occur because of misunderstandings and miscommunication. Once the children really see why the other did something or said something, the conflict often just vanishes. Many fights happen between children because they don't see one another's worlds. Often when one child really sees that he has hurt the feelings of another he will cry with remorse.

One morning Don and Tim got into a heated fight. They were actually best friends who often chose one another as partners in the awareness game. The sensitive love and caring between the boys in their relating to one another was very obvious. I was surprised to see them so upset with one another, although I knew that often children who were closest to one another also fought the most. These boys, however, seldom raised their voices to one another. I called the boys together for Creative Conflict. If a conflict involves only a few children and not the whole class I usually deal with it by having just those individuals share. That day I gave the rest of the class a quiet reading assignment so I could get on with Don's and Tim's conflict. The rest of the children knew that they were welcome to come and help resolve the conflict if they wanted to, and a few boys chose to come and help.

We started with a short centering meditation. Don, who was the most upset, expressed his feelings first. Don complained that Tim had taken his money out of his desk and put it in his own desk. He expressed how he came in from recess and became scared because he couldn't find his money. I asked Don to share his feelings with Tim. He said, "It scares me when you take my money and put it in your desk." It was now Tim's turn to mirror back Don's feelings. He became very stubborn and wouldn't talk. I put my arm around Tim and asked if he was upset because he was only trying to help Don. Tim opened up and said that he put the money in his own desk because it was falling out of Don's and he wanted to keep it safe for Don. He couldn't tell Don why he had done it because Don had already gone to recess. Don was asked to mirror Tim's expression. Don, even though he could mirror Tim's words, namely that Tim had taken the money out of his desk as an act of caring, didn't show caring back to Tim right away. Tim had had a very distraught look on his face during most of the Creative Conflict, and this seemed to be disturbing Don. He said to Tim, "I don't like it when you make those faces, like you are right now." Tim mirrored Don. I asked Tim if he made those faces when he was upset. He said "Yes". I asked Don how he felt about Tim now. He responded, "I feel OK because I know he didn't take my money on purpose but was saving it for me and I know he's not making those faces at me on purpose." I then asked Tim how he felt about Don. He said he felt Don didn't care about him anymore. Don immediately said, "Yes, I do, Tim." Then in a soft voice he said, "I'm sorry." The air was clear. Don saw how he had misunderstood Tim's intention in putting the money in his own desk. Tim forgave Don for misunderstanding him. Tim and Don began to laugh and talk playfully together with Eugene and Anthony, the two boys who had come to help. The conflict was over.

There are nine guidelines listed in the book *Creative Conflict: Learning to Love with Total Honesty*, written by Christopher Hills and published by the University of the Trees Press (1980). These guidelines are very useful in the resolution of conflict. Basically, they are guidelines for working on the ego. Most of the guidelines are too hard to explain to younger children but I use them in an intrinsic way in the process.*

One guideline the children use easily is guideline number six called "Red Herring."** A red herring is an irrelevant statement or comment which is way off the point and which can take a Creative Conflict on a detour in a fruitless direction and waste time.

---

*Upper-grade children can discuss the guidelines and can actively use them.

**Origin of terms: In hunting, a red herring was dragged across the path of the quarry to distract dogs away from the scent of the animal so they couldn't chase after it.

One afternoon we had a discussion on how it feels to not be living with one or even both parents. (I had several students who lived in foster homes and many children from divorces.) The discussion was very emotionally charged, the children being very open with their feelings. Suddenly Anna spoke up, "Last night I went to the Board walk and I saw Jeannie there. We went on the roller coaster together." The Boardwalk is a great attraction for children in Santa Cruz County and I knew a whole sharing about adventures at the Boardwalk now could easily emerge, drawing the children away from the vulnerable heart sharing they were already in. I told Anna that her bringing up the Boardwalk in the middle of a discussion about how some children fel being separated from their parents was a red herring because it took everyone's thoughts in a new direction. I suggested she share her feelings about the Boardwalk with her friends at recess time, and brought the discussion back to the original topic.

Sometimes in the middle of a Creative Conflict a child will bring up another conflict which is totally irrelevant to the conflict at hand. This is another type of red herring which only takes the energy away from the real problem. I remind the child that we are resolving the conflict at hand and that if he would like help with the second conflict he may have help at another time. The children I have worked with become very sharp in picking up one another's "red herrings". After awhile they even begin to pick the teacher's "red herrings" during lessons. It really keeps you on your toes.

Another guideline I find especially useful with children is guideline #1: "You are whatever disturbs you". Often children get very angry and upset with another child's shortcomings because they see in the other their own problem, and they can't stand looking at their own problem in another. This is what guideline #1 is all about. If something disturbs a person about another, it is often because that person has or used to have the same problem. It is not always easy to help children to see that they need to point the finger inward and look at themselves in this way. They tend to point the finger outward and blame the other. I find that patience, gentleness and persistence help children best to look into this mirror of life. If a child can't see the mirror and is totally resisting, I find it best to drop the issue and come back to it at another time. The same conflict will surely arise again where the child is disturbed by another's problem which is also his own. Gradually over time the child will be able to see that he has only been seeing himself in another. When this happens, a wonderful clearing of the psychic atmosphere occurs between the two children. They often become friends.

Sharon and Jeannie had the type of conflict which exemplifies the guideline, "You are whatever disturbs you". Jeannie, a new student, joined the class in November. Almost immediately she began to have conflicts with Sharon. Both girls were very sweet and helpful in class and tended to be responsible. At the same time they both had another side to their personalities which came out in their relationship to one another. Sharon came in crying at lunch time one afternoon claiming that Jeannie was mean to her. Sharon was upset because Jeannie had asked Sharon to give her some of her lunch in what Sharon claimed was a mean voice. I called Jeannie into the classroom and we sat down to resolve the conflict. First we did a short centering meditation. Sharon was asked to express first. She looked at Jeannie who was sitting knee to knee with her and spoke up, "I didn't like the way you talked to me in a mean voice when you asked me for some food." I said, "How did that make you feel, Sharon? Can you tell Jeannie?" "It made me feel mad," Sharon responded. Jeannie was asked to mirror Sharon's feelings, which she did accurately. It was now Jeannie's turn to speak. She expressed to Sharon, "I talked to you in a mean voice because you gave Mary some of your lunch but you wouldn't give me any." I asked Jeannie if she could tell Sharon how this made her feel. She said, "It made me feel bad, Sharon, like you don't like me." Sharon was able to mirror Jeannie. She felt bad that she had hurt Jeannie, and she agreed that she would share some of her food with Jeannie the next time she shared with Mary. Jeannie then said that she wouldn't talk to Sharon in a mean voice anymore, and the girls ran off to play.

Several days later Jeannie came in in tears during lunch hour, expressing that Sharon had spoken to her in a mean voice. Here was the same conflict arising again, only the roles were reversed. In calling the girls together I learned that Jeannie had cut in front of Sharon in line to use the swings. In Creative Conflict, Jeannie expressed to

Sharon, "I didn't like the way you asked me to get out of the line in a mean voice." What was disturbing Jeannie about Sharon? Jeannie herself had just done the same to Sharon a few days before. I gently led her to see this. I led Sharon to see that she had just treated Jeannie the way she herself did not like Jeannie treating her. In talking to one another in an unkind manner the two girls were mirror images of one another. They were disturbed when the other did the same thing they themselves did. I had them both mirror the point I was trying to make to be sure they understood. By their response it seemed that they had. This conflict did not arise again between the girls. In fact, I don't recall doing much Creative Conflict with them during the rest of the year. One of the wonderful things I find in using Creative Conflict in the classroom is that once a conflict is totally resolved through this type of communication, it does not often arise again. This seemed to be the case with Sharon and Jeannie's conflict. Not all conflicts between children are this easy to resolve, however. Some take more time and persistence on the teacher's part. Sometimes you can only go so far and you have to let the children have some time to work on the conflict on their own. For example, one afternoon out on the playground, Mary said something unkind to a four-year-old boy visiting the school with his mother. When asked to do Creative Conflict with the boy, she was unwilling to talk to him or look at what she had done to him. I gave her a few hours to think about what she had done. When I checked with her several hours later she was now willing to acknowledge her behavior and to share with the boy. The mother of the boy seemed appreciative of the way the conflict was handled.

Sometimes during a Creative Conflict, the children deny what they are really feeling or they act as if they don't hear what is being expressed. Then later on, they show by their actions that they have indeed heard. This happened often enough that I learned to trust that children were hearing, even though they appeared not to. To illustrate, one afternoon I came upon Roger and Brian fighting outside the classroom door at recess time. Both boys were kicking. Roger had a hold on Brian's hair and was pulling it. They were both really into it. I quickly grabbed each of them and pulled them apart. I led them into the classroom and had them sit knee to knee on different pillows. After a short centering, each boy was given a chance to express what had happened. It turned out that Roger had chosen to go to the library and draw during the recess time. Brian had told Roger that he himself would never go to the library to draw and that, as far as he was concerned, it was a stupid thing to do. Roger got angry at Brian's comments and started to kick Brian, and soon they were into a full-fledged fight. I encouraged Roger to express how Brian's comments made him feel. "It made me mad." Brian was asked to mirror Roger's feelings. He then expressed how he felt it was stupid for Roger to go to the library and sketch. At this point I realized Brian must have some expectation of Roger which made him not want Roger to draw. I asked Brian if he was jealous because Roger was drawing or if he was saying these things to Roger because he really wanted Roger to come outside and play with him instead of draw. Brian denied that he had any such feelings. I then asked the boys how they could fix their friendship now that they had hurt it with a fight. They shared that they wanted to tell one another they were sorry and shake hands. I aked if they felt the problem was solved. They both responded, "Yes". They walked out to recess together. Brian grabbed a piece of paper, deciding to draw with Roger. In the Creative Conflict process itself Brian denied that he was in any way upset that Roger was drawing, but because he was asked about it, he had a chance to get in touch with what was really going on inside himself. He had heard my question and was able to realize that he could be with Roger by choosing to draw with him. In this way children do not always work out a problem to completion in the Creative Conflict process itself but, because of the process and deeper sharing, are able to make choices in their lives which create more harmony for themselves and others around them.

As I said before, I usually only did Creative Conflict with the children who were involved in a conflict, giving the rest of the class a quiet work assignment as well as inviting those who wanted to help with the conflict to join in. Children become restless after awhile if asked to sit for a long time and listen to another's conflict. Thirty children are too many for this type of process, unless the conflict has to do with all thirty children. Such a large number can be intimidating to the children and they may not open up as readily and risk their self-images. Groups of six or less are ideal, creating intimacy and security, so that the children become more willing to open up and share.

One morning Monica and Anna had a spat as school began. It started when Anna asked Monica, "What are those bumps all over your skin?" Monica had a strange looking rash which her father had explained was an allergy. The bumps covered every inch of her body. Monica began to cry when Anna mentioned her spots. Since the class was already together as a group I proceeded to have the girls express their feelings with the whole group present. Monica expressed how Anna's asking about the bumps made her feel bad because she already felt ugly because of the bumps. Anna was asked to mirror Monica's feelings. In her mirror Anna showed that she heard Monica. Anna said that she hadn't meant to hurt Monica's feelings but that she had felt curious about the spots. She looked at Monica and quietly said, "I'm sorry." Both girls were shy about sharing their vulnerable side with the whole group present. Monica felt too intimidated to work the conflict out to completion in the group so I sent them outside to further their discussion alone. They solved their problem successfully in about five minutes and returned to class, quietly joining into the classroom flow. Ideally it would have been best to have called the girls together for their Creative Conflict alone or in a very small group. The size of the group made it too difficult for them to feel comfortable enough to totally share their vulnerable selves.

I have found at other times, however, that the larger group can help children be more honest. Ultimately, the teacher has to tune in to the children and feel out what's best in each situation. I had a group of third-grade girls the last year I taught in the public schools who had a very difficult time listening to one another, often holding solidly to their ego positions and not being able to mirror each other. One afternoon two of the girls—Rochelle and Noni—were fighting after lunch. Two crying, angry girls entered the classroom. In this case I chose to keep the whole class together for the Creative Conflict. It turned out that Rochelle had promised to eat with Noni and then ate with Jill. Noni had called Rochelle names. Knowing how difficult it was for Noni and Rochelle to give up their ego positions, I decided to begin by leading the class in a somewhat extended meditation. I presented many questions in the meditation for the children to think about: "How do we solve a problem once we are into it?" "How do we solve a problem without saying it's the other person's fault?" "How do we not blame the other, saying it's his or her fault, without saying she caused it—she is the bad one?" After the meditation all three girls looked calmer and brighter. At first, Rochelle did not want to discuss the problem in front of the class, but something told me it was best to keep the whole group together where the girls would know that what they were expressing would be heard and seen by others.

So, being aware of the girls' listening problems, I decided not to start right away with Creative Conflict. Instead, I asked them to come up with their own solution to the problem. Rochelle suggested that they tell one another they were sorry and shake hands. They all agreed that they wanted to do this. In good humor they shook hands and said, "I'm sorry." They then returned to their places in the circle. I then challenged Rochelle for promising to eat with another and not following through with her promise. Noni expressed to Rochelle how she felt about being left out. Rochelle was able to mirror Noni and see how she had hurt Noni's feelings. Later that night in bed I reflected on how much the girls' change of mood from anger to cooperativeness was due to the long meditation and how much was due to the fact that the girls were in front of the whole class. Conflicts between these girls were usually not this easy to resolve. I decided both factors had helped. It seemed the group energy had supported the girls in working out their conflict. Alone they probably would have held on much longer to their ego positions because these girls were aggressive and expressive, unlike Anna and Monica who were shy and reserved. Rochelle and Noni did not want to look bad in the group for not sharing and not being cooperative.

In working with the conflicts of these particular girls all year long, I discovered something else important about doing Creative Conflict with children: you run the risk of the children using Creative Conflict to get attention. Before Christmas I spent a lot of time doing Creative Conflict with Danielle, Noni, and Rosa—three leaders of a larger group of girls who were always getting into fights. Conflicts arose daily over their calling one another names, writing uncaring notes, giving one another subtle put downs, and calling one another after school to say unkind things. At the same time they were friends and always chose to play with each other. I found myself spending much time doing Creative Conflict with them, including many recesses and lunch hours. It became very frustrating because often, after I had spent large chunks of time working with them, using mirroring and other listening techniques, they would go out during the next recess and do it all over again.

For example, Danielle visited Rosa's house one evening and they decided to call Noni. Rosa called Noni and said, "I know who you are and I know what you did". Noni recognized Rosa's voice and was hurt and angered by Rosa's communication. I spent half an hour helping the girls mirror and listen to the extent they were able to. Later in the day another conflict had arisen between the girls. What I didn't realize was that the girls were using the Creative Conflict to get attention and it had become an energy drain for me. Often after doing Creative Conflict with them, experiencing their continual non-listening and non-caring, I would go home drained and discouraged to the point of tears. As mentioned earlier, Danielle and Noni had very hard egos to penetrate. Danielle would never look at the fact that she may have helped create a situation and would often respond by saying, "but she did such and such". Noni seemed very thick-headed and was not willing to change her uncaring behavior and attitude toward others. During the Christmas break, being away from the class, I got in touch with how much energy drain the girls were. I decided to stop doing Creative Conflict with them.

One afternoon, shortly after Christmas break, Noni came in complaining, "I have a problem with Rosa. She called me a bitch." I responded, "I am no longer going to help you with your problems, as my help doesn't seem to be helping you change. You'll have to solve it yourselves." An interesting thing happened. As soon as I began to have the girls work out their own problems, they had far fewer problems. There was a sharp decrease in unkind behavior between the three girls and I found that I had much more creative energy to share with the rest of the students and to put into teaching.

A typical example of a problem these girls created happened after Christmas vacation. Danielle invited Noni and other girls to her birthday party. Her mother told her she had invited too many girls and she couldn't have them all come. So Danielle told Noni she could no longer come. Noni's mother called Danielle and told her she wasn't very nice. Danielle came in the morning wanting me to solve the problem. I told her that her mother and Noni's mother would need to solve the problem, as they helped to create it. I didn't get sucked in. You may be wondering why I was not working more with the girls' parents to help resolve such conflicts, especially since the parents were directly involved. Earlier in the year, I had contacted the parents but found them to be even more hesitant to look at themselves than their children were. It was the attitude of "I know my sweet daughter could not have done that. Surely it is the other girl's fault." I realized early on that the parents would not be much help and that I was essentially on my own.

In my experience, most children do not use Creative Conflict for negative attention as these girls did but come from a genuine space when bringing up a conflict or problem. Bill and Roger used Creative Conflict in a positive way to keep their friendship clear. Both boys were capable of some pretty intense fist fighting, hair pulling and kicking. But after awhile, instead of physically hurting one another, they would come and wait outside the classroom door until I came along to help them solve their conflict. It was not uncommon to hear Bill say, "It happened again, Miss Herzog. I got mad at Roger and threw him down." I could often tell that while waiting outside the door, they had already solved their conflict to some extent by talking, and it began to take less and less time to help them resolve their differences. One afternoon, I found myself chuckling over the way they chose to let me know they needed help. They both came in after lunch, angry with one another over a disagreement at recess. They came in and put their chairs back to back, sitting so they would not have to look at one another. I called them over to the rug and their conflict was quickly resolved. I never found Creative Conflict with Bill and Roger to be an energy drain. Quite the opposite—it was always good to experience their willingness to be open with their feelings. One gauge to help judge whether the Creative Conflict has become an energy drain or not, is to tune in to how you feel at the end of one. Do you feel enlivened or drained? Another is to ask yourself the question, "Are these children growing from the Creative Conflict? Do I see them growing in their ability to resolve conflict? Do I feel their willingness in the Creative Conflict process?" If the answers are yes, then you can continue with the Creative Conflict process with the children.

Many of the children quickly come to see and appreciate the honesty and integrity Creative Conflict brings to their relationships. They are sometimes quite moved by having a chance to express themselves and really be heard. This happened to a boy named Mark, a boy from the classroom next to mine who had a conflict one day at lunch recess with two girls in my class. I invited him to join us in Creative Conflict, making sure it was all right with his teacher that he participate in our class for awhile. He had never done Creative Conflict before. I led the children through a short centering. Each child in turn—Mark, Tami, and Eve—expressed their feelings. Mark was upset with Tami and Eve for calling him names. Tami and Eve were upset with Mark because he had pulled their hair. After all feelings were expressed and cleared, Mark returned to his class. Later that same afternoon, Mark came and asked if he could play dodge ball with our class. He joined our game with a smile. The next day he came after school to visit and talk with me. He had never done so before. We had not had any real contact with one another previous to the Creative Conflict. The open sharing of feelings and respectful listening to one another in the Creative Conflict had spoken to Mark's being. Perhaps it was the first time he had been heard in this way. He now felt connected with me and the children in my class, and he often came to visit us throughout the rest of the school year.

In doing Creative Conflict with the children when one child is hurt by another, I often ask the child who did the hurting if he has ever been hurt in the same or a similar way to the child who is hurting. When children can recall their own hurt, it becomes much easier for them to understand the pain of another, and they often become more willing to take responsibility for what they have done to another. I used this technique in a conflict between Anthony, Dennis and Danielle one afternoon. Danielle had taken Anthony's ball, Anthony had hit Danielle on the legs with a bat, and Dennis jumped on Anthony, trying to stop him from hitting Danielle with the bat. After they had shared their versions of what had happened, I said, "Let's talk about your feelings". I asked Anthony to speak first. He looked at Danielle and said, "It made me really mad when she took my ball". Danielle mirrored Anthony's feelings. I then asked Danielle if she ever felt like Anthony. She shared, "Yes, the kids in my class last year always used to grab the ball away from me. That used to make me angry". She then looked at Anthony and told him she was sorry for taking his ball. Because she had gotten in touch with her own hurt, she was better able to see how she had hurt Anthony. I asked Anthony if he was satisfied that Danielle understood how he felt. He responded, "Yes." As we discussed in this way, I could feel the tension between the children dissipating. I could actually feel the energy leave the room. Danielle then shared with Anthony how she felt when Anthony hit her with the bat. Anthony mirrored her. I asked Anthony if he had ever been hit before by another student. He was able to get in touch with an incident the week before when Roger had hit him with a stick. I asked him if he could now see how Danielle was feeling. He responded that he could and apologized for what he had done. Anthony was then asked to tell Dennis how he felt when Dennis jumped on him, and Dennis mirrored him. By now all negative tension was gone between the children. Dennis said, "All I really want is to be friends with you, Anthony". They both agreed that's what they wanted, and they decided to play four square. They invited Danielle to play but she chose to do something else.

In the sunlight.

CHAPTER 16

Let Them Shine

Over the years I have found that in general children do not tend to share much about school with their parents. As one parent described it, "It's like pulling teeth to try to find out what's happening in school." Even children who love their teachers and their school experience, do not share much of it with their parents. Parents often come to the teachers to find out what's happening at school because they just can't get their children to talk about it. Often they are surprised to discover how much is actually going on in their child's classroom. One of the few things my children did bring home in my first six years of teaching was the songs they were learning. They did not share them directly with their parents, however, but usually would sing them as they went about doing other activities. Their parents would overhear them singing and would then mention to me how much they liked what their children were learning to sing.

For this reason I was quite astounded when my students began to tell me that they were teaching their parents, brothers and sisters and even at times grandparents how to do centering. One half to three quarters of the children began to share with me either incidents in which they taught someone to do it or used it on their own at home. I had not expected this to happen. Here are a few examples of the types of things the children would tell me about how they had taught their families at home.

Rochelle—"My mom does centering with me. One time I was teaching her how to do it. I kept peeking at her. She kept her eyes closed. I had her imagine she was a whale in the sea. She said it felt good."

Karen—"My mom thinks centering is real nice because I did it to her when she was sick and she felt a lot better."

Don—"My sister had a stomach ache. I told her to relax her body and breathe in and out and then imagine her stomach ache feeling better. It's sort of fun when you're a teacher to your little sister. She felt better. She said, 'That really works.' My mom said, 'Mmm, I've got to listen to this.'" Don's mother became very interested in the centering process after Don brought it home. She came to school shortly thereafter to find out more about it. She was especially interested in trying it with Don's ten-year-old sister who was somewhat hyperactive.

Why were the children taking the centering process home, not just on the level of talking about it but on the level of teaching it and doing it, when they took so little else of their school experience home? I believe they did this because centering spoke to their hearts and souls, to their total being. I do not think they were aware of why they shared it. Centering made them *feel* good, made them feel more whole and secure, more worthwhile as beings living on the earth, so they just naturally wanted to share this experience with others. They wanted the chance to commune on this deeper level not just at school with their classmates and teachers, but with their families as well.

How often have you heard children express that they are bored or don't know what to do? Some children found centering an answer to this problem, because through centering they discovered the world of inner images, colorful impressions, feelings and pictures which they could tune to in those seemingly boring moments when there was no outside stimulus to keep their minds occupied. Rick said, "I use centering when I'm going to bed and when I don't have anything to think about, and it helps me. I do it and then I think about something, like I'm a tree or the best baseball player. Sometimes I pretend I'm a camel and all these animals."

Bill expressed a similar experience, "My dad was playing his stereo. I felt bored, so I went outside in the moonlight. I imagined I was jumping into the water and playing at the beach and having fun all day. It was fun." Mary said, "I use centering sometimes when there is nothing to do on rainy days. I wish it was snowing. I go to my room and sit on my bed and relax myself and then I feel better." Sharon also liked to use her imagination when she had nothing to do. She told me one afternoon, "I do centering when I get home from school and sometimes at nighttime. I imagine I'm a feather or a raindrop turning into rainbow colors. In December I imagined I was a Christmas tree and people were decorating me. I feel fine after doing centering. My favorite is imagining I am an Easter egg where everybody picks me up and puts me in a party."

Karen, a quiet eight-year-old girl with soft brown eyes, told me, "I do centering every night before I go to bed and every morning when I get up. At night, I pretend that I am a star because you can see stars out of my window. In the morning I pretend I'm the sun. It makes me feel good. It makes me feel warm inside." These children no longer had to rely on situations or relationships with others for their happiness. They were freer human beings. They could now look to their own inner resources, their own imaginations and minds for their enjoyment. To be able to play and find fulfillment in one's own world of rich images is a natural part of childhood, which some of our children today miss because of television and too many commercially made toys and too many scheduled activities. Centering helped these children rediscover that self-sufficient part of themselves.

I found that some of the boys had discovered the fantastic power of their imaginations to condition reality while playing in soccer and baseball games. At home in their rooms before the games on Saturday mornings, they would do centering, and they started this practice on their own. They found that by using their imaginations to visualize themselves playing well they could actually perform better on the ball field. Stewart was a dark-eyed quiet eight-year-old boy. His mother said that Stewart used centering before baseball games because he believed that projecting success helped him to achieve it. Stewart related the experience to his mother: "It just helps me do well."

Rick, a very sweet, shy eight-year-old boy, told me, "Sometimes I do centering before games like soccer. Before the games, I imagine I'm going to do good. Sometimes I don't have time to do centering before games. It feels different then. I play better when I do centering. I pass better and shoot better. I can see the difference. I can feel it, too. Sometimes Stewart and I do centering together before the games."

Tim said, "One night, a Friday night before a soccer game, I couldn't go to sleep because I was thinking about the soccer game and then I did centering and I imagined I could go to sleep and I could have a good soccer game and score a goal. Then in the morning I put my clothes on and went to the soccer game. I bet my mom an ice cream that I would score three goals and I did. Centering gave my feet energy to kick the ball."

I was especially surprised when Al shared a similar experience, because Al never said anything in class in response to centering and I didn't think he liked it. But he told me one day that he used centering to help himself before soccer games. He said that centering helped him score all four goals for his team in one game and told me how he helped his team win a trophy. He was beaming.

All of these boys were quite serious as they spoke. They had a sense of conviction and confidence in centering, which was amazing for their young age. What had they discovered in it? They had discovered that through their imagination they were able to project something positive into the future, they could be masters of themselves and the situation they were in. What would happen if children were taught centering all through their school years? Perhaps they would attain a sense of confidence which would carry through the whole of their lives. Perhaps they would bring true conviction to all they had to tackle and face in their lives, even very difficult tasks.

It amazed me how many ways the children, on their own initiative, applied the centering techniques, without my having suggested it. For example, many children used it to put themselves to sleep at night. I find that insomnia is more and more frequent among children and they will often tell you, "I feel sick; I didn't sleep last night." The main cause for it seems to be that they cannot relax. Since the centering process begins with relaxation, it is a natural thing for them to try. Here are some of their experiences:

> **Tina**—"Sometimes I tense my body real tight and then I get sleepy and fall asleep."
>
> **Stewart**—"When it's in the middle of the night and I can't sleep I relax my body and keep on relaxing it until I fall asleep."
>
> **Bill**—"I use it when I can't sleep. I try to get the thoughts out of my mind, like when my dad gives me something like a new cereal and I can't wait to get up in the mornings, I lay down and squeeze and relax. It makes me relax more, then I relax my head, then my eyes close."

One brother and sister used it together: "First I tell one body part to relax, then Jerry says one, then I say another one. Then we tell stories. Then in the morning we remember our dreams and talk about them."

Through centering the children were able to gain control over emotions, anxiety, boredom, and many states of mind which face most of us throughout our lives. They did it with a simplicity and ease which was a lesson for those of us who have not yet learned how simple life is, once we learn to draw upon the incredible inner resources which are nearer to us than breathing, closer than hands and feet. Could it be that the ancient scriptures were only trying to give us this one truth—that there is a power inherent in each person, all we have to do is learn to use it.?

Centering became a real avenue of bonding for some parents and children. It became a lifeline for the heart, a connection of love which did not exist before, a merging of the parent's and children's deeper souls. This happened to Anna, a sweet quiet seven-year-old and her mother, Theresa. Theresa was not a stable person and, although she had a nice heart, she often hid it beneath a nervous and talkative exterior. At home when under pressure she became very bitchy with her husband and children. In fact, several husbands had left her and, during the second year that Anna was in my class, the husband that Theresa had recently married separated from her. With all this going on and the need to support her family financially, Anna's mother became sharp and impatient with her children. This would always cause her pain afterwards because she deeply loved her children and this was not at all the way that in her deeper heart she wanted to treat them. Anna loved her mother very much. She yearned to spend more time with her mother who had to spend much of her time at work. Her mother's angry fits caused her deep pain and loneliness.

Anna brought centering home to both her younger brothers and her mother, teaching them how to do it. Anna began to ask her mother to lead her in the centering experience. But in order to lead Anna in centering, Theresa had to lift herself out of her own pain temporarily and tune more deeply into her daughter's world. Anna loved these experiences. They became real moments of closeness with her mother, moments closer, deeper and more precious than any bedtime story or bedtime kiss could have ever been. It was as if they had been lifted temporarily out of life's challenges so that their spirits could meet together for a short repose of tranquility and joy. In order for Theresa to lead Anna in centering she had to enter her deeper, more vulnerable heart, the heart that Anna was thirsty for. Here is what Anna said about her mother, "In the morning and at nighttime my mom leads me in centering. Sometimes my mom says it to help me get up in the morning. She has me imagine I'm a butterfly or a horse. It feels real good to have my mom lead me in centering. I love it."

My original vision in teaching meditation to children was to open up the dormant part of the brain which Dr. Rozman spoke about when she first came to my school district to speak on meditation. Little did I know what real effects it would have on the children's lives. Little did I realize how much they would make centering part of their daily lives and that they would, of their own accord, with no prompting from me, bring it home to their family and friends. The level of maturity with which they did this was often quite astounding.

Because of centering and the sharings we had afterwards, the children began to share with me more about their personal experiences with centering and as a result I began to see what their home lives were like. In previous years, all I knew about them was what happened in the class but now I was coming to understand them on much deeper levels.

Jason was one of the children whose parents were gone at night. He wandered the streets at night alone, even though he was only eight years old. He hid his insecurities by being overly nice to adults, so I found him very sweet, and for a long time I had no idea what his home life was like. He gave me a clue into it when he told me how he used centering to help himself fall asleep at night. Being an eight-year-old in a family of teenagers, he was often forced to fend for himself. One morning he told us, "I do centering every night when I can't get to sleep because the T.V. is on too loud and my brothers' radio is on. I do centering real hard and try not to hear anything. It's like I am tuning out and I can't hear anything. Then in the morning I do centering again, but it's the other way around. I hear stuff and then get up." Even though Jason and other students didn't advertise the difficulties they were having in their home lives, these momentary glimpses into an entirely different reality of their lives caused me to give them even more love than before.

Remember Roger, the little boy whose hamster died before school began one morning? Roger's family was just the opposite of Jason's. Roger and his mother began to use centering as part of their nightly story time routine. First Roger would lead his whole family through centering. Then everyone would listen with eyes closed as Alice, his mother, read a bedtime story. In his sharing of the experience one morning I could feel the warmth and caring which flowed between Roger and his family. "I say, 'relax bodies' to my mom and dad and sister. Then mom reads us a story as we keep our eyes closed. When mom read Pegasus I saw a horse with wings flying in my imagination. It was fun. It feels like you are doing centering by yourself—like no one is there." Alice also shared with me how warm and wonderful these family sharings were and how much they meant to the whole family.

Knowing these things about Roger's life at home not only brought me closer to him but helped me to understand him. It was ironic that Jason, whose home life was terrible, was so sweet in class, while Roger, whose home life was nice, used to pull people's hair out. Yet this was in fact a common occurrence with children. It was as if the children whose homes were not happy needed to create a safe, peaceful place for themselves at school, while the children who were well-behaved at home used school as an outlet for their other energies.

Roger had a reputation as a "bad boy", not only with the teachers but also with the other children. When he was angry, he would throw rocks. One day I said to his mother, "Roger isn't bad. He has this anger problem to work on, but his real being isn't like that; it's very sweet. Especially after centering or after Creative Conflict, so much love and caring comes out of him." His mother cried. She said, "No one ever said that to me about him before." She shared with me that he had this naughty streak since he first began to walk. We talked about it for a long time. I felt the problem was deep-rooted, maybe an inborn trait of his basic personality that every child is born with. Knowing this led me to realize I had a real responsibility to help him master it because if I didn't, he would probably carry it through his entire life. So I began to work with the school counselor, and we set up a program which allowed Roger to feel good about himself whenever he controlled his anger. By the end of the year, Roger had gained enough self-mastery over his problem that he began to communicate his feelings by talking about them, saying, "I'm angry with you" instead of throwing rocks at the other children or pulling their hair. The deep anger problem in Roger was really a problem at the soul level. The reason I felt this was that the pattern was so uniform. No matter what kind of thing made him angry, even an accident, he would always take it personally and always resort either to the rocks or the hair pulling. According to his mother, he was pulling out the hair of two-year-olds even while still a toddler. Knowing his parents and how they raised their children, I saw that there was nothing they did that would have made him that way. His sister had no problems of this kind at all. The mother was neither too mothering nor did she give the children too much freedom. There was a nice balance in that home between the children having love and having responsibility. So I felt that Roger was born with this trait. Just as the beauty of the pearl is hidden beneath the cover of the shell at the bottom of the sea, so the child's inner beauty may require some work in order to bring it to light. All of us have patterns to master and qualities to change about ourselves in order to refine our beings and bring out their natural luster. Perhaps this is the true purpose of life.

Meditation, Creative Conflict, and awareness games all nurture this unfolding of the soul.

Afterwards . . .

On November 17, 1981, I attended a parent-teacher meeting for the small private school where I now work. It was held at a restaurant in Scotts Valley. As I placed my order, a young voice at my side said, "Hello, Miss Herzog." I looked into the sweet, calm, deep, blue eyes of Anthony. He had grown taller over the three years since I last saw him. As we conversed it became obvious that he had maintained the centered self-confidence he had gained three years before. It felt as if no time had passed at all. Anthony's face radiated the same warmth and joy it so often did following a meditation. Like Roger, Anthony had had a reputation for anger and fighting. Something had polished his soul very bright to make it shine. And I knew when I looked into those eyes that it would shine for the rest of his life.

Letters from the Parents
and the Administration

Several weeks before this book was due at the printer I ran into the parent of a child who had been in my class the first years I taught centering meditation to the children. I shared with her that I was almost finished writing a book about those years at Brook Knoll School. She said that the two years her son was in my class were the most peaceful school years her son had ever experienced, and that she felt the centering had helped him slow down to the extent that he was able to develop beautiful handwriting. After talking to her the idea came to me that it would be nice to have a special section in this book called "Letters from Parents and the Administration." So I called up my former principal and some of the former parents of children I taught. Here are their letters. All of these were written from three to five years after their children had experienced centering in my classroom.

Ward M. Stewart
Principal

It has been my pleasure to work with and to know
Stephanie Herzog for several years as her Principal at
Brook Knoll School. She is a uniquely sensitive individual.

I observed Stephanie utilizing simple centering
techniques with easily observable results in many of her
students. We did not study Stephanie's results scientifically,
but the majority of observers felt there was a remarkable
difference and increase in students being able to attend to tasks.

Sincerely,

Ward M. Stewart,
Principal

March 19, 1982

Dear Stephanie,

Marc's second and third grade years with you were really good ones for him. He has always been very lively and your centering activities helped him get into the right frame of mind to do his school work.

I noticed when I helped in your classroom that it was quiet with a relaxed and comfortable atmosphere. I was especially pleased that you did not need to raise your voice to get the children to do what they were supposed to do.

Marc's schoolwork, and handwriting especially, were excellent in the third grade, I believe, because he was encouraged to work carefully and because he felt comfortable in your classroom. Marc is in the eighth grade now and I've noticed that when he's been in classes that had a noisy and pressure-filled atmosphere, Marc's handwriting and other work were not as good as they should have been.

It would have been a good thing for him as well as the other children in his classes if they had the benefit of the centering and meditation activities that you did with your classes on a daily basis.

Thank you again for the two happy years Marc spent with you.

Fondly,

Karen Darocy

Karen Darocy
March 23, 1982

Dear Stephanie,

My son Kevin tells me that two of his best years in school were second and third grade where he took part in your program of Centering. He tells me that Centering helps him relax and also take control of stresses and problems at that time.

I think it's a great program and would like to see it implemented in more schools. Best wishes for continued success.

Maeve Harris

Maeve Harris

March 18, 1982

Dear Reader,

Our son, one of Stephanie's more "active" students as a 2nd and 3rd grader made sure he resisted all of his teacher's efforts to teach him to "get in touch with his feelings" and release physical and emotional tension with her "centering" technique. Five years later, however, much to his surprise, he found himself using his former teacher's method of relaxing his body and focusing his concentration and energy while participating in an aikido class!

Our daughter was a much more willing student of meditative arts and practiced Stephanie's centering method very frequently in her everyday life. Studying with Stephanie at the age of seven and eight (she was in her class for two years), Lori routinely meditated before bed each night to prepare for a sound and restful sleep, and used this method of achieving perfect relaxation to direct a positive energy flow to others in need.

The first experience happened the night our little dog Chester was poisoned and lay rigid on the couch as though rigor mortis had set in. I was frantically trying to reach the vet on the telephone. Upon returning to the family room, I found Lori very peacefully cradling the stiff, little body in her arms. She quietly reassured me that Chester would pull through, saying "He's going to be okay, Mom, I know it because I gave him all my good energy and he can feel that I love him."

She was right. Half way to the vet's that night, he regained consciousness and was restored to normal health. I think she will always feel partially responsible for his recovery and I'm inclined to agree with her!

The other experience I vividly recall is the day Lori's great-grandma was to be in surgery. She and her brother were scheduled to be on an airplane bound for Disneyland at the same time grandma was to have her serious operation. I hadn't been aware of Lori's deep concern in this difficult situation until at departure time she said to me, "Mommy, tell me what time Grammy's operation is so I could send her good energy from my airplane."

Suzanne Meschi

Boulder Creek, CA

March 20, 1982

Dear Readers:

My son Kelly was in Miss Herzog's class in the 2nd and 3rd grade. She taught the students to find their inner self, and brought the students closer together.

Kelly has been with the same classmates throughout grammar school. They show respect for each other and have a special bond between them.

Sincerely,

Mrs. Peggy Goetz

March 19, 1982

Dear Stephanie,

I was pleased to hear that the publishing of your book is in the near future.

Bill and I feel that Nick was very fortunate to have you as his teacher for the second and third grades. First grade was a bad experience for Nick, leaving him without self-confidence. Your teaching techniques, including the use of "centering", marked the growth of Nick's self-confidence. Today, Nick's self-image is very good. He is the first to remark that centering was the beginning of his positive attitude.

Again, our thanks to you and much success with your book.

Fondly,

Pamela Whitstone

March 19, 1982

Dear Stephanie Herzog,

Thank you for introducing Jackie to "centering" at a young age. Initially, Jackie was hesitant about closing her eyes and using the technique. However, before the semester was over, Jackie was "centering" in and out of the classroom. She especially used it to relieve her boredom on long car trips. I think "centering" helped Jackie academically, psychologically, emotionally and spiritually. It would have helped my oldest child so much if he had a teacher who used "centering."

Jackie's exposure to your technique awakened our entire family's interest and we have all used it since you taught Jackie. I would love to see this exercise and discipline of "centering" included with the three R's in school so people might learn to make it a routine like brushing their teeth. Can you imagine the heights we human beings would attain physically, intellectually, psychologically and spiritually?

Sincerely,

Marian Disperati

Marian Disperati

March 18, 1982

Dear Stephanie,

Our son Hunter's second and third grade years in your classroom at Brook Knoll were very beneficial to him. It opened up his sensitivity and awareness to others in the class and on the playground.

One of the centering's greatest benefits was exposing them to their own feelings and the release of any tension. Hunter can always calm himself by centering.

Sincerely,

Joan Dunn

Joan Dunn

March 18, 1982

Dear Reader,

Our son was quick tempered verbally and physically. "Bouncing off the walls" was a label given to him in pre-school. He had Stephanie as a teacher for both 2nd and 3rd grade. In her classroom he learned a way to control himself effectively from within.

I remember one particular occasion when he got very angry at his younger sister. He ran up to his room and slammed the door. I waited for the customary yelling and throwing things, but it never came. After a few minutes I checked on him. He sat crosslegged, eyes closed, palms up on the middle of his bed. I asked, "Are you okay?" "Be quiet, Mom" he said, "I'm centering."

He had many challenges on the playground but none in Stephanie's classroom. He is in the 6th grade now and has had many ups and downs in different classroom and playground situations.

I believe Stephanie's ideas and methods are useful and effective. Parents might also benefit from similar education. Our son's greatest behavior and academic strides since 2nd and 3rd grade have come when he has been in calm, controlled non-threatening environments. Some classrooms provide this; others do not.

Another class activity of Stephanie's I appreciated was when each child was given the opportunity to be "child of the day."* Each of the other children said something that they liked about that child. Stephanie wrote down the responses and sent them home. Those were the first positive responses that ever came home to us about our boy. We read them aloud at the dinner table. He asked to have them read again and again.

Thank you Stephanie!

Martha A. Bedal

Martha A. Bedal

*This was a variation of the "love circle" exercise from the book, *Exploring Inner Space*.

Biography of Author

Stephanie Herzog has been instrumental in introducing new methods of teaching reading, meditation, and awareness activities in the classrooms of the Scotts Valley Elementary School District in California and has helped lead many "Meditation With Children" seminars at the University of the Trees (Boulder Creek, California) since 1977. She is currently head teacher and teacher trainer at University Community School, an elementary school dedicated to the development of holistic education located near Boulder Creek, California. University Community School uses the methods outlined in this book.

Stephanie received her B.A. (cum laude) from the College of Notre Dame (Belmont, California) where she was elected a life member of Kappa Gamma Pi, the National Scholastic and Activity Honor Society of Catholic Women's Colleges. She earned her California Standard Life Elementary Credential through the College of Notre Dame. Ms. Herzog, after several years of original research in holistic education studies and development, received her Master's from the University of the Trees in Transpersonal Education.

Other books for educators and parents available from University of the Trees Press

Meditating With Children: The Art of Concentration and Centering

A leading handbook that teachers and parents use to develop their child's concentration and creative imagination. Excellent results with gifted, retarded and hyperactive children. For pre-school through high school. Especially designed for classroom or working with groups of children. 160 pgs., $5.95. Deborah Rozman, Ph.D.

Meditation For Children

Gives the teacher or parents a deeper understanding of what meditation really is and what it can do for children. Special application for the family. Also instructions and guide for making conflict creative. (Published by Celestial Arts and Pocket Books). 160 pgs., $5.95. Deborah Rozman.

Exploring Inner Space

Exciting games which open not one but seven fantastic levels of human potential; imagination, intuition, memory, emotions, intellect, social awareness and the physical body and its senses. Easy to use in the classroom. These games will add a whole new dimension to any curriculum and are a lot of fun. Good for pre-school through adult education. 480 pgs., $9.95. Christopher Hills, Ph.D. and Deborah Rozman, Ph.D.

Creative Conflict

A process to help resolve conflicts between children or adults which really works. Seven steps to real listening and communication. A must for every classroom. 324 pgs., $5.95. Christopher Hills.

Nuclear Evolution

A book of vision and a unique book of knowledge which reveals in depth the structure of human consciousness. Shows you how to use your powerful imagination to bring great changes in yourself. 1024 pgs., $12.95. Christopher Hills.

Rise of the Phoenix

The author's original research into the seven brains of man makes especially exciting study for junior high, senior high and adult education classes. Includes a chapter called "A New Method of Learning" which will inspire the teacher looking for something totally new. 1014 pgs., $14.95. Christopher Hills.

Meditating With Children Cassette

This is a selection of delightful meditations from Deborah Rozman's books including the favorite "Spaceship Meditation", read by the author herself. For all ages. 1 hr., $8.00. Deborah Rozman.

Joy in the Classroom Cassette

Meditations recorded live in the classroom by the author. Children's discussion and personal sharings from meditation included. Includes "The Heart Meditation", "Rainbow Meditation" and two science meditations. For all ages. 1 hr., $8.00. Stephanie Herzog.

Uncle Alf's Circus

This is a highly imaginative cassette tape of children's special meditations. It speaks to the child's heart with such guided imagery topics as "Uncle Alf's Circus", "The Cuddly Teddy Bear" and "Animal Chanting". Recorded live. 1 hr., $8.00. Christopher Hills.

Beginning Meditation Tape

The first steps in learning to meditate. Gives an understanding of the process and instructions on how to do it yourself. 1 hr., $8.00. Deborah Rozman.